DATE DUE

NOV 1 1 1994	NOV 0 3 1998
NOV 1 9 1995	APR 1 1 1999
NOV 1 6 1996	
JUL 5 1997	
NOV 2 8 1997	
JUL 1 5 1998	

GAYLORD   PRINTED IN U.S.A.

SURVIVING NATURAL DISASTERS

How To Prepare for Earthquakes, Hurricanes, Tornados,
Floods, Wildfires, Thunderstorms, Blizzards, Tsunamis,
Volcanic Eruptions, and other calamities

by

Janice McCann and Betsy Shand

WITHDRAWN

DIMI PRESS   Salem, Oregon

DIMI PRESS
3820 Oak Hollow Lane, SE
Salem, Oregon 97302
© 1995 by Janice McCann and Betsy Shand
ISBN: 0-931625-26-2
Printed in the United States of America
First edition

Library of Congress Cataloging in Publication Data;

McCann, Janice.
    Surviving natural disasters : how to prepare for earthquakes,
hurricanes, tornados, floods, wildfires, thunderstorms, blizzards,
tsunamis, volcanic eruptions, and other calamities / by Janice
McCann and Betsy Shand.
        p.   cm.
    Includes bibliographic references and index.
    ISBN 0-931625-26-2 ; $14.95
    1. Natural disasters. I. Shand, Betsy   II. Title
GB5014.M39   1995
613.6'9--dc20   94-25256
                                                     CIP

Thanks to:

Bruce DeRoos—Cover design
Dennis Pashby—Illustrations
Lynne Mac Vean—editorial comments
Vern Cope, Dave Silver, and Jeff Kresner—sound advice
Dr. Steven M. Cassidy, Professor in the School of Business,
        Howard University, Washington, D.C.,—insurance

8 Ciro 4/2/99- 6/99

CONTENTS

INTRODUCTION

In all regions of the world, we are subordinate to many powerful and destructive forces of nature. The monumental events created by natural phenonema are facts of life and they can cause loss of life and property. At their worst, disasters wreak havoc, destroy communities, and cost millions.

We cannot control the weather. The barometric pressure, the velocity of the winds, and the humidity that make up our atmosphere are way beyond the reach of mortals. We can only observe these phenomena. We cannot dictate how the earth orbits and moves within itself. We can't stop the massive shifting and colliding of the plates under the ocean or the volcanic eruptions that boil in the Pacific Ocean's 'Ring of Fire'. The volcano explodes into a firestorm of molten lava, the tsunami's monster wave bursts and topples from the deep and the hurricane pounds its pelting winds and rivers of rain. Suddenly we are engulfed in a state of emergency.

Thousands of our neighbors are overwhelmed at once. With rescue services overworked, survival will depend on preparedness and self-sufficiency, especially in the first 72 hours of a disaster. It will be critical to know what to do if confined to your home, perhaps cut off from other family members. Whether we face an earthquake or a thunderstorm, the time to get ready is before it catches us in a state of unreadiness.

The purpose of this book is to show how to protect your family and minimize damage to your home. It will provide simple safety guidelines to help you prepare for and cope with natural disasters in your home, community, state, and country or wherever your travels take you.

THE DISASTERS

Some disasters are a result of volatile weather conditions. These are: thunderstorms, blizzards, hurricanes, cyclones, typhoons, tornados, wildfires, and floods. One disaster can beget another, as when a thunderstorm generates lightning that ignites a forest fire or a hurricane produces torrents that spawn a flood.

Other disasters are of the earth movement type. These are: earthquakes, volcanic eruptions, and tsunamis. When the earth moves, fires and floods and landslides can result.

A general preparedness plan will include a suggested list of insurance questions, a family plan, and supplies to store.

We will identify the geographic regions, characteristics, and seasons of each disaster. Before, during, and after will be presented for each main event.

This book deals only with sudden natural disasters. Other calamities, such as insect invasions, droughts, oil spills, nuclear accidents, improper toxic waste disposal, etc., are beyond the scope of this book.

GENERAL PREPARATION

The key to meeting the challenge of any natural disaster is preparation. Prevention is not possible. Through advance planning and development of necessary survival skills, we can dramatically increase the odds of surmounting any disaster. In our scenario, the family comes together in a spirit of anticipation and takes control as a unit by evaluating potential danger, making decisions, and obtaining training to face what is no longer the unexpected.

Since advance notice will usually not be given in the event of a natural disaster, preparedness must be adopted as a daily way of life. General preparedness is a positive attitude which precipitates achieving actions.

Getting ready involves simple tasks such as storing canned goods, water, and camping supplies, bracing chimneys that could fall on the house, and testing smoke alarms twice a year. Making copies of favorite family photos and storing them for safekeeping, calling the school for information on fire drills and evacuation plans, keeping valuables and important papers in a safe deposit box, contacting a friend or relative outside the area to relay messages in time of emergency, teaching the children how and when to dial 911 and keeping the car's gasoline tank filled are all ways of working towards good general preparation.

Following are sections which will aid you in getting ready for any event from a thunderstorm to a tsunami.

PLANNING

OUT-OF-THE-AREA
CONTACT PERSON

In any disaster, telephone service will be limited to 911 and medical emergencies and it may be impossible to call across town to check in with friends or relatives. Even though communications are cut off at the local level, it will still be possible to call out of the immediately affected area on long distance.

You will need to choose a friend or relative who lives far enough away from your geographical location to be unthreatened by the disaster for which you are preparing. If you live in the United States in California where earthquakes are predicted, you may want to choose an out-of-state contact. If you live in Hawaii where volcanos are active, you will want to choose someone on the mainland. If you are threatened by hurricanes on the Atlantic seaboard, you will want a contact who lives further inland.

The contact person will serve three purposes:

First, to relay information about the well-being and location of other family members with whom you have lost touch during the disaster.

Second, to store copies of your important documents and family photographs and send them as needed.

Third, to provide third parties such as rescue workers or insurance representatives with vital medical and statistical information. In a life and death emergency, the contact person could also act on your behalf to give your heirs necessary information on banking, medical, and insurance matters. You may want to designate medical power of attorney, including your living will, to your contact in case you or other family members are incapacitated.

OUT-OF-AREA CONTACT
PERSON INFORMATION

Following is a suggested list of information you may want to provide for your contact person. A copy of this list can also be included in your emergency supply kit, including the name, address, and telephone number of your out-of-the-area contact person.

- Your name and address

- Your children's full names and birthdates

- Color of children's eyes and hair

- Children's mother's and father's name

- Children's sex and race

- Children's heights and weights

- Children's scars and birthmarks

- The name, address, and telephone number of your children's daycare or school and person in charge.

- Children's pediatrician or physician and phone number

- Children's other identifiers (glasses, braces, etc.)

- Your children's fingerprints and current photo graphs

- The name and phone number of your children's sitter

- Your family physician and phone number

- Blood types for everyone

- Social security numbers for everyone

- Dates of birth for everyone

- Home and work telephone numbers

- A list of any special health problems, allergies to medication, and prescriptions for everyone in the family

- Your attorney's name and phone number

- Your bank, branch, contact person, telephone number, and checking account number

- Your savings account or Certificate of Deposit number, branch location, and phone number

- Your safety deposit box number and location (copy of the key can be included in your parcel of important papers)

- Your homeowners insurance company, policy number, agent, and phone number

- Your life insurance carrier, policy number, agent, and phone number

THE FAMILY PLAN

A family plan is very important in preparing for a disaster. Everyone in the household is included in the preparation, from helping locate a safe place to be during the disaster to getting ready for the aftermath by gathering supplies and water to store. Call a household meeting and devise an emergency plan. By preparing ahead, you will be working together as a unit to reduce trauma, ensure survival, and minimize injury and property damage.

FIRST AID TRAINING AND CPR

Disasters can cause injuries. Lives can be saved with a timely response. Learn what to do and how to administer aid by signing up for a first aid course and CPR training at the Red Cross or YMCA. Your church, school, or community center will also be a good prospect for this instruction. Emergency preparedness videos are available at the Red Cross and can be borrowed for home viewing. Watch together as a family and open a discussion. This will give children an opportunity to express fears, ask questions, and quell anxieties by being told about what could happen and what can be done before, during, and after.

EDUCATION

Knowledge is a powerful tool. Follow newspaper and television accounts of disasters. Visit the library and read up on the disaster that threatens your geographic area. Being informed on the history and causes of these occurrences will give you perspective and understanding of the natural phenomena. Your children will be studying disasters at some point in school. Use the opportunity to talk about what could happen and how to be ready. Reeducate yourselves when reviewing procedures and checking and restocking supplies.

A SAFE PLACE

Walk around the house to find a safe place to be during the disaster, such as a closet, a basement, or a hallway away from glass, top-heavy furniture, and flying objects. Practice bracing your legs and back against opposite walls while seated flat on the floor and protecting your head with your arms. Practice being a small target. Practice the Red Cross "duck, cover, and hold on" technique by getting under a heavy table or a desk. If children's play areas are located where the children might be hurt, relocate those areas as necessary.

UNDER THE BED

One-third of all your time is spent in bed. The probability of the disaster hitting when you are asleep is high enough to consider what to do if suddenly awakened by a disaster. In order to be ready, put together a small box or gym bag of practical shoes and clothing, heavy gloves, and a flashlight for each person in the household to store under his or her bed. You may want to have both sweats and shorts to cover all the seasons. If you are surprised in the night, you will be ready to suit up and react.

FIRE DRILLS

You can prepare for fire by stocking and learning to use frequently tested fire extinguishers, to be placed in the kitchen, basement, with emergency supplies on each level of the house, and in cars. Have each qualified, responsible family member learn to use the fire extinguisher. Make a point of checking fire extinguishers every six months and replacing them with new equipment if necessary. Another essential safety device is the battery-powered smoke alarm. These warning systems are inexpensive, easy to install, and required by the fire marshal. Alarms should be installed wherever family members are sleeping at night, outside bedroom doors, in hallways on every floor of the house. Be sure to check alarm batteries at least once a year.

As part of the fire awareness plan, discuss and practice fire emergency steps. For instance, it is advisable to sleep with bedroom doors closed so that, if a fire starts, no one will be easily overcome with smoke. Closed doors also set up a barrier to flames. If either an alarm sounds or you smell smoke, the door can be felt to see if it is hot. Do not open the door first. If the door feels hot, keep the door closed and roll a wet towel up to stuff in the crack under the door. This technique will keep the smoke and flames away while you escape through another exit. Exits should be planned in advance, and materials should be kept on hand in the room. Under the bed is a readily accessible storage place. These items might include a rope ladder for escape through a second story window, a towel and water in a plastic jug. Another technique to practice is crawling low on the floor to avoid smoke inhalation. The smoke from a fire is a danger in itself and many people are suffocated in fires in this way every year.

The Red Cross "stop, drop, and roll" techniques are also useful in training family members how to react if actually caught on fire. The way to put out the flames is to stop in your tracks; avoid instinctively running away as it will fan the flames and feed it more oxygen. The next thing to do immediately is to drop to the ground flat, then roll over and over on the floor until the fire is out. Regular practice of fire drills is recommended by the Red Cross to prepare your family to react quickly and to escape danger.

FIRE DRILL SUMMARY

- Store towel, water, rope ladder under bed.

- Plan exits.

- Conduct regular fire drills.

- Install smoke alarms.

- Check fire extinguishers.

- Sleep with bedroom doors closed.

- Feel doors before opening.

- Put damp towel in door bottom to block smoke.

- Crawl low on floor.

- If on fire, drop to the floor and roll.

- Leave by pre-planned exit.

WATER ACCESS AND PURIFICATION

Do not drink tap water, as it may be contaminated in an emergency. Safe water is stored in the refrigerator in the form of ice cubes. You can also use water from the toilet tank if no bluing or other chemical treatment agent is present. Do not use water from the toilet bowl. The tank water can be purified by boiling for 5-10 minutes.

Water can also be harvested from the hot water heater, provided the glass liner is intact or the broken glass can be well strained. We do not recommend trying to strain out broken glass shards as they can be extremely minute and cause internal damage when ingested. First turn off the gas or electricity going to the hot water tank. Either turn on a hot water faucet inside the house or open the valve on top of the tank. Then place a clean jug or other vessel under the tap and fill it up with water. Refill as necessary.

UTILITIES

During the family meeting, walk around the house together and take a tour of the utilities and appliances that may be damaged or need to be shut off after the disaster. Locate the tools for turning off the water main at the street and practice turning the water off inside the house and at the main line. Become familiar with the gas shutoff tool and main line as well. Check the circuit breaker box or fuse box and practice turning electrical power off and on. Be sure panels are correctly labeled for each section of the house. Keep spare fuses and flashlights next to the boxes. Consider storing the tools needed right next to the main utilities or furnace for easy access. Spares can be kept in the emergency kit or with neighbors.

MEETING SPOTS

Decide where to meet after the disaster. Know where the family will reconvene. Hide a house key in an agreed-upon spot in case family members miss contact.

CHILDREN'S NEEDS

You can help reassure your children by having them pick a cuddle-buddy such as a teddy bear to talk to before, during, and after the disaster. Sharing their fears will help them overcome the trauma, especially if you are not there. This is the time to prepare them for a possible separation. Let them know you will be home as soon as it is safe. Tuck a family snapshot in with the cuddle-buddy.

Disasters strike suddenly and are frightening and confusing for everyone, especially children. Disasters interrupt daily routines that children depend on. If they know what to expect and what to do, children will be much less traumatized by such an event. Your children will need your guidance on how to prepare before the disaster as well as how to respond when it hits and afterward.

The development of a family plan and bringing everyone together to open a discussion and create a system of preparing, responding, and surviving as a group is a crucial step in alleviating children's anxieties. Children can help prepare and store supplies for the disaster. They should know who their out-of-area contact person is and how to phone them. Help children pack their under-the-bed emergency kits and include the cuddle-buddy, family snapshots, and other small items they choose.

Contact your local emergency management and civil defense office or the Red Cross to find out what disasters to prepare for in your community and to get the information, including videos, to share with the whole family.

Teach children about warning system sounds. Test smoke alarms, fire alarms, horns, and sirens in your home, neighborhood, and community. Have children watch or help install and test smoke alarms and practice what to do in a fire drill. Demonstrate how your child can call for help and when they should do so. Familiarize children with 911 and other local emergency numbers and post these numbers on every phone. If children can't read yet, educate them to the emergency symbols for fire, ambulance, and police. If you have a programmable phone, input these numbers and use the symbols to identify them.

Children should memorize their family name, address, and phone number as soon as possible. Very young children can carry I.D. cards and give copies to babysitters or day care workers.

You can help reassure your children after the disaster, while seeking assistance or housing. Keep children with the rest of the family as much as you can. One worry that children suffer from is that the parents will not return and this can produce anxiety. You will want to calmly explain what you know about what is happening and where you all will be staying together. When talking to children at this time, it is most reassuring to meet them at their eye level by kneeling or squatting down. Encourage them to talk about the disaster and about their feelings. Listening to them will help the adjustment process. Involve the whole family in such a discussion if possible. Children should have active ways of helping as well. Give them chores so they can work on the family's recovery. They will feel that they are a part of the solution and that things will be getting better and back to normal through these tasks.

Anxieties and fears will come up and you can help your children understand the causes of their discomfort and reassure them that conditions are temporary and will normalize eventually. You will give your children an example of how to act by the way you react in this emergency. If you exhibit panic and fear they will forecast continuing danger and be afraid that the event will be repeated. The fear of injury and death combined with the fear of being left all alone is very real for children, whether it springs from the imagination or not. Recognize your childrens' need to feel safe. Stay calm and in control. Tune into your children's emotional needs once the physical danger is past. Ask your children to explain what is troubling them and open a healthy, healing dialogue.

FAMILY JOBS

Delegate after-the-disaster jobs in advance so that each family member knows what to do and can act quickly. Delegate according to ability. Children may be placed in charge of comforting contained pets and feeding them or of keeping their belongings together in their under-the-bed kit.

First aid will be the first order of business, to be administered by qualified family members. After injuries are treated, the other tasks will follow. Prioritize, beginning with putting out fires and checking for gas leaks. Immediate evacuation may be necessary in some cases. Work from a check list to assign jobs. Any disaster cleanup may involve stepping in a lot of glass, rubble, or water and mud. It is important that everyone be properly outfitted in sturdy shoes and protective clothing.

SCHOOL PLAN

How safe are the school buildings where your children attend classes? You will want to ask a number of questions about the structure of the building itself and about the disaster preparation procedures in place. Here are some sample questions:

Has the building recently passed an official fire and safety inspection?

What are the limits of the liability and medical coverage on the school's insurance policy?

Does the building have an up-to-date sprinkler and fire alarm system?

Does the building have a well-stocked basement shelter in case of hurricane, tornado, or other storms?

Is the school away from the flood plain?

Is the building earthquake safe? If it is an older building, have seismic retrofitting adaptations been made?

What, exactly, are the emergency and evacuation plans? Where are the exits and what are the routes? What transportation will be used?

Who will be in charge and what qualifications and experience do they have?

Are food, water, and supplies are available on site?

What medical personnel will be standing by? Does the school nurse have adequate supplies to treat a lot of injuries at once?

Is a Red Cross or Fire Department disaster expert available to speak at the school and offer training for parents and students?

Is there a backup generator to run the heating and electricity?

Are disaster and fire drills conducted regularly?

If kids prepare an emergency supply pack with flash-light, canned fruit, energy bars, a cuddle-buddy and family snapshots to keep at school, where can it be kept?

How and when will parents be contacted after the disaster?

ELDER CARE PLAN

How safe is the structure where your older parents, grandparents or retired neighbors live? If they are housed in a retirement or nursing facility, what are the emergency procedures, evacuation and relocation plans? If you find the situation inadequate you may want to make a change of venue for the better, whether to your own mother-in-law's apartment or to a newer, nearby apartment building with good structure and planning. Following are some suggested questions:

Has the facility recently passed a building, safety and fire inspection?

How comprehensive is the facility's insurance and liability coverage and what are the dollar limits for medical coverage?

Is the building away from the flood plain?

Does the building have a well-stocked basement shelter in case of a hurricane, tornado, or other storm?

Is the building earthquake safe?

If it is an older building, have seismic retrofitting adaptations been made?

What, exactly, are the emergency and evacuation plans? Where are the exits and what are the routes? What transportation will be used?

Will ambulance or rescue helicopter units be available as needed?

Who will be in charge and what qualifications and experience do they have?

If this is a hospice or nursing home how will patients be evacuated and what facility will they be transported to?

How do the resources of the evacuation facility compare to the present facility in terms of meeting specialized medical needs?

Is the blood supply safe?

If hospitalization is required, how will the patient be transported and where is the hospital? Are ambulances and life flight helicopter rescue units readily available? Does the facility have its own transportation?

What notification will be given and who will have access to the patient? Are there forms to fill out now?

Is a Red Cross or Fire Department-sponsored speaker scheduled to speak and offer training for residents, patients, and relatives?

What food, water, and supplies are available on site?

Is there a backup generator to run the heating and electricity?

Are disaster and fire drills conducted for staff and residents?

Are medical supplies stored on site?

How and when will relatives be contacted after the disaster?

Are there relevant forms and paperwork to fill out in advance and is legal advice available on such matters as medical power of attorney and living will advisories to physicians?

PET PLAN

There are a number of steps that you can take to

ensure the well-being and survival of your pets, livestock, or farm animals.

It is very important to make your animals identifiable so they may be returned to you when lost during a disaster. Cats and dogs can wear collars and I.D. tags with their name, your name, current address, and phone number.

Another way to help you locate pets, particularly cats, after the disaster is to be aware of the places they like to hide around the house or yard.

Dogs should be licensed. Always be sure to keep all vaccinations current. In a disaster, pets will become frightened and agitated. Keep pet carriers and leashes on hand so that the animals can be contained and calmed. A pet carrier should be big enough to hold a towel, litter box, and a bowl of water, in addition to your pet. Store the pet carrier with an additional towel or blanket to cover the carrier once your pet is inside. Always approach frightened animals with caution as they may become aggressive. If animals have not been contained during a disaster, on returning they should be contained or leashed before letting them close to people.

Emergency shelters do not allow animals. You will want to plan ahead for other places to take your pet such as a friend's or relative's outside the disaster area. Some holding areas for pets, livestock, and farm animals will be set up after the disaster via emergency services, and this information will be broadcast on the radio following an event. Some hotels will allow pets for a small fee and you may want to call ahead to know what is available in your area. Store pet supplies, carriers, food, water, and towels with your emergency supplies.

NEIGHBORHOOD PLAN

Get to know your neighbors by calling a meeting. Ask the Red Cross or Fire Department to come to the meeting to talk on disaster preparedness and emergency training. Make a list of all neighbors by resources, expertise, and special needs. Use a checklist to record names, addresses, and phone numbers of neighborhood doctors, nurses, plumbers, cellular phone owners, portable generator owners, physically impaired individuals, and elderly people. Record the children, their ages, and their pets from household to household. Include which homes are supplied by natural gas. Designate backup help for water and gas and electrical shutoffs so that if one neighbor can't shut off his gas, his next door neighbor will. Make sure everyone knows the location of their special tools and the correct shutoff procedures. As in the family plan, make a general overall plan so people can be located after the disaster.

Following the disaster, you might try using the signal ribbon system. Every household is given three ribbons of different colors to tie on the front door or other visible spot to indicate the condition of the residents after the event. Use white for "everything is fine", yellow for "we're o.k., but need some assistance" and red for "emergency – injuries". This system allows the neighbors to broadcast visually to each other to identify priorities without physically going on the property in question. Emergency crews can benefit by this system as well.

Check on emergency plans for elderly neighbors. With apartment building dwellers, inquire about the structural safety of the building. Ask about procedures, drills, and fire equipment that could save lives in a disaster.

Are supplies on hand on site to meet special needs? Make sure wheelchair access and exit procedures are in place for those who need it. Know who needs dialysis, oxygen, physical therapy, special medication, or any medical monitoring. Ask who is an outpatient and what kind of treatment they undergo and how often.

Help older neighbors prepare food, water, and supplies that they may need for an emergency. Help install smoke alarms, lightning rods, cut down threatening trees, check circuit breakers and bolt down hot water heaters and bookcases. If the living situation is inadequate, bring the relative home where emergency needs can be met by other family members.

THE BANK PLAN

You will need access to funds and to your safety deposit box for important papers, insurance policies and appraisals after the disaster. Some suggested questions for the bank to answer are as follows:

Is the bank architecturally sound, even disaster proof?
How safe is it? Is the building earthquake safe?

If the building is older, have seismic retrofitting adaptations been made?

Has the structure recently passed a building, safety, and fire inspection?

Is the building away from the flood plain?

What are the bank's emergency procedures?
Are drills conducted on a regular basis?

Who is in charge and how may they be contacted?

How will you get your money and how will it be safeguarded? Is the bank Federally insured? What are the dollar limits for each account and safety deposit box?

How and when will you be contacted regarding your accounts and investments in a disaster?

INSURANCE

Is your homeowner's insurance adequate to cover your property and assets if a disaster strikes? Disaster insurance rescues the policyholder from catastrophe.

Even if you do not presently have disaster insurance, you may find it affordable in lieu of unreimbursed catastrophic loss in a traumatic time. There may be a moratorium on disaster insurance in your area if there has recently been a state of emergency. The time to shop for coverage and get on the waiting list is now, before another occurrence. Following are some sample questions to open a dialogue with your insurance agent:

SAMPLE QUESTIONS

What does my homeowner's policy cover?

What disasters does it cover?

What disasters do I have to prepare for in this geographic location?

What is the deductible?

Is my claim calculated on what I owe on the house or on the appraised, or current market, value?

Is my house insured for the full value of the mortgage or replacement value, whichever is greater?

How much insurance should I have to get full payment for my losses from my insurance company?

Am I insured for replacement value of my property, belongings, and valuables?

What is my medical limit coverage? What is the limit for injuries? Who does it cover?

If there is a moratorium in this area on disaster insurance, when may I get on the waiting list and when will policies start being written again?

What if my home is not up to current building code?

Will I pay more in premiums for a masonry home? For a home on stilts?

Can I get a building ordinance rider which will cover up to 50% of the costs of upgrading my home should it have to be rebuilt?

How much will the rider cost per year? Per month?

How does the insurance company determine loss of use?

Does a loss of use mean that my transportation and lodging costs are covered if my home is unsafe following a disaster? Does that mean I can stay in a hotel after a disaster and charge it to my insurance?

What dollar limit, if any, is there on loss of use?

What kind of inspection would I need to get in order to determine the structural integrity of my home?

Does the insurance office have an engineer available to inspect structures after the disaster?

What does the term dwelling extensions mean?

Does it apply to my decks, fences and unattached structures?

What is the formula for calculating dwelling extension limits?

Are my shrubbery, trees, hedges, and landscaping insured? For how much?

In case of an earthquake, is an aftershock a separate incident?

What if there are aftershocks months after the event?

Do I need a separate policy for fine art and antiques?

Do I need a floater policy for camera equipment, computers, jewelry, and furs?

Will my flood insurance cover me if my house was
built in a flood plain?

Will my homeowners policy extend to my
automobile and my safe deposit box?

If I am forced to evacuate, will my policy remain in
force, even though the premises may be
unsecured?

Considering that theft is a problem after disasters,
is taking reasonable precautions to prevent it a
factor in insurance claim awards?

Will I need an appraisal in order to guarantee
replacement cost on heirlooms and antiques rather
than "garage sale" cost?

Do you have an appraiser to recommend?

Do I need a rider policy for plate glass?

If I have disaster coverage, will it deter or exempt
me from emergency assistance at the time
of a disaster?

Does earthquake insurance cover other earth movements, such as volcanic eruption, or landslides?

Does it cover tsunamis?

Is it possible to obtain tsunami insurance if I live right on the beach?

Is damage done to my home by a disaster tax-deductible?

Can I tax-deduct a property loss in either the year of the loss or in the prior year if the loss is in a disaster area declared by government officials as warranting federal assistance?

Is my car covered by my homeowner's policy if it is in the garage at the time of a disaster? If not, can my car insurance cover the damage?

Is damage done to my car tax-deductible if caused by a disaster?

Is damage done to my trees or shrubbery by an earthquake, hurricane, tornado, flood, fire, or other sudden event tax-deductible?

If my neighbor's house catches fire as a result of a disaster, spreading the fire to my house, or if an explosion occurs, am I covered?

If I had to demolish my home in a disaster area or relocate, may I claim the loss even though I wasn't directly affected by the disaster?

If my property wasn't damaged by the initial disaster, but is now in danger of resulting mud slides and I am forced to sell or evacuate by authorities, may I claim the loss?

DOCUMENTATION FOR INSURANCE CLAIM

If you suffer a loss of personal property, you will be expected to provide sales receipts or a professional appraisal and videotape or photographs of your belongings. Insurance companies rely on this evidence to settle claims.

1. SALES RECEIPTS

These verify the date and cost of your purchase. Cancelled checks, credit card slips and copies of contracts are all good proof. Copy your receipts and store copies in your emergency kit, safe deposit box, and with your out-of-the-area contact person.

2. PROFESSIONAL APPRAISALS

It will be helpful to have appraisals for valuables that you do not have receipts for, such as furs, antiques, fine art, heirloom pieces, gifts, collections, and jewelry. Have the appraiser provide you with a written, dated inventory and statement of value.

Appraisers' charges vary and your insurance agent may be able to recommend one. Appraisals can be done in your home. For portable items such as silver, jewelry, crystal, and china, your local jeweler or antique seller may be the place to go. You need not pack in all the pieces, as a fork or a wine glass or a serving plate should do to establish the pattern and give you a base value.

Keep copies of your appraisal(s) in your emergency

kit, in your safe deposit box, and with your out-of-the-area contact person.

3. VIDEOTAPE

Some insurance agents will provide videotaping service to their clients. They will come to your home to make a tape for you, at little or no charge.

Video cameras or camcorders can be rented from local video stores. Practice using the camera at the store before taking it home to become familiar with the loading and unloading of the tape, holding and maneuvering the camera, and techniques like panning, close-up shots, and zooming.

Make a video of all of your possessions by walking through your home room-by-room, including closets. Pull valuables, such as furs and tapestries out of your closets and lay out on beds. Lay out jewelry and silver on a table or countertop to make close-up shots being very careful to be in focus. Turn pottery and china over to film the artist's signatures and trademarks. Go outside and record your home's exterior and landscaping.

Camcorders also record sound. Narrate as you go,

giving purchase date and price of purchase of individual items along with a little history on each one. The latter is especially helpful with antiques and gifts.

4. PHOTOGRAPHS

For insurance purposes, color photographs are more effective than black and white photographs. Descriptions, dates, and prices can be written on the back of the photos. Update your photo inventory as you add to or subtract from your personal property. Be sure to have copies made, sent to your out-of-the-area contact person, and stored in your emergency kit and safe deposit box.

STORAGE OF IMPORTANT INFORMATION

Now that you have your household inventory and a videotape or photographs, a safe storage place should be established. You will need both a local, accessible place and one out of the area. In case disaster strikes, your long distance documents are out of harm's way. Have the video tape copied or have copies of photos printed and put these duplicates in your emergency kit and in the mail to your out-of-the-area contact person. Store the originals in your safe deposit box.

THE INSURANCE COMPANY PLAN

In the pandemonium caused by a disaster, how will your insurance company be set up to respond to the claims of its policy holders?

Will tents be erected in the middle of town, or are there other provisions for temporary shelters?

Will you be given a voucher to stay in a hotel if your house is wrecked, or will cash be immediately available to feed your family?

How much documentation or on-site investigation will be necessary before your claim can be settled?

What will happen if you have no videotape or any immediate records?

What will happen if you have been forced to evacuate and don't have your policy in hand?

EVACUATION

Although evacuation may be viewed as the last resort, it is sometimes the best solution. All disasters can cause evacuation for at least some segments of the affected population. When the alternative is loss of life, evacuation is the only choice. The disasters most likely to necessitate a quick exit are hurricanes and other volatile storms, floods, tsunamis, earthquakes, volcanic eruptions, and wildfires. Every family plan should include an evacuation plan, just in case.

Situations may arise when your own observations will tell you to enact your plan, even before officially ordered to evacuate. It is important to trust your own judgment and act decisively. For example, when you see the flames of a wildfire burning the prairie below and whipping up your hill, it is time to run. Take your stored emergency provisions and leave. When thunder has accompanied a deluge of rain for days and the nearby river boils over the banks, it is time to enact the plan. When the earth shakes beneath your feet, when the volcano or tsunami warnings are broadcast, or when the dark skies and swirling winds signal a tropical cyclone, it is time to survive. You must be prepared to evacuate if lives are endangered.

The evacuation plan will include having a destination such as the home of a relative or friend not living in the affected area, a shelter, or a motel. Escape passages out of the house will have been predetermined and procedures for reuniting the family will also be in place. Several alternate routes for both driving and walking will have been mapped out ahead. An out-of-the-area contact person will have been chosen so that family members can communicate and important medical and insurance information can be provided. Supplies will have been stored in emergency locations in easy-to-carry gear such as backpacks and garbage cans with roller wheels. You will be more self-sufficient if you are able to carry some possessions and supplies with you, particularly if you are in a remote area.

Government aid is potentially available in distressed areas, and a sometimes state of emergency is declared. Any major event is a priority for services to affected communities. The Red Cross will set up first aid stations including food, and shelter facilities, although this may take up to three days following the disaster. In the interim, prepare to be on your own. Insurance companies may be of immediate help. Full insurance coverage is always the best defense against loss of property and loss of use. After a disaster, your insurance company may issue cash or vouchers for food, lodging, transportation, or other immediate expenses from a temporary base of operations in a central location. Although it is best to have your policy information and proof with you, conditions may present a relaxing of demand for formal documentation in the first strike of a disaster.

Following is a list of conditions under which to evacuate:

CONDITIONS FOR EVACUATION

- Uncontainable interior fire

- Encroaching wildfire

- Explosions

- Gas smell indicating leaks and possible explosion

- Flooding

- Asbestos leakage (from popcorn ceilings, wrapping on furnace pipes, furnace ducts)

- Landslide

- Unstable, shifting ground

- Collapsing buildings

- Tsunami warnings

- Typhoon warnings

- Tornado warnings

- Volcano warning

HAZARDS

Earth movement disasters such as an earthquake, tsunami, volcanic eruption, or landslide will shake, rattle and roll you, your home, and your property. Hurricanes and other storms can cause the same kind of devastating displacement and damage. Trees and chimneys may topple and fall on houses, power lines short-circuit, gas lines and water mains erupt. The structure of the house itself may be compromised from the foundation up, causing floors to slide apart, porches to separate, and garages to collapse. Pruning overhanging trees, supporting chimneys, and bracing the structure can alter the risk of damage to your property.

In such occurrences, danger also exists inside the house from shattering mirrors and windows, falling furniture, toppling bookcases, and flying pots and pans. Safety can be greatly enhanced by applying safety film to windows, skylights, mirrors, and glass doors. It will not keep glass from shattering but it will keep it in place in the window or door frame. Some grades of safety film used for security purposes are capable of withstanding the force of a hurtling boulder. Safety film will also protect you against the elements and intruders. Bolting down heavy furniture and bookshelves to wall studs, putting safety latches on cupboard doors, bracing refrigerators, securing hot water heaters, installing flexible hose on gas appliances, moving heavy objects to lower shelves, and eliminating anything that could fall from above the bed are easy and inexpensive ways to secure your home.

Following are a list of suggestions for eliminating potential hazards.

EXTERIOR HAZARDS

1. TREES

If large trees could fall on your house you may want

to consult an arborist as to the health of the trees, the importance of their rooting systems for soil stability, and the danger posed in terms of limbs which may need pruning to prevent falling. If you are on a very steep slope, you may want to consult a civil engineer as well. Be sure to check the proximity of tree limbs to power lines leading into the house or outbuildings. Prune limbs that could crash into power lines in turn shorting them and causing a fire.

2. CHIMNEY

Chimneys pose a threat to your safety in a disaster. The height and weight of the chimney will determine the power with which it will fall if inadequately braced. The higher up off the roof line the chimney is positioned, the harder the fall. Brace ceiling joists under the chimney with plywood to keep chimney bricks from breaking through the roof if the chimney falls. Current building codes require external bracing to strengthen chimneys. You might consider obtaining bids from licensed, bonded contractors to find out if your chimney meets acceptable local standards, especially if you are in a seismically sensitive area. You may also want to have a chimney sweep clean the creosote out of your chimney at least once a year to protect against the danger of flue fire.

3. POWER LINES

While in your yard check the location of power lines that may fall during the disaster. Advise your family and neighbors of the danger and avoid these areas later.

4. WATER, ELECTRIC, AND GAS SHUTOFFS

Know the location of the shutoff valve inside your home and know where to turn off the water main at the street. Have the necessary tool to turn the water off. Turn the valve as far as it will turn to the right, clockwise. Practice shutting the valve off and on in order to become familiar with it. If the main valve sticks or is frozen, call the water company to come out and give it a lubrication treatment. This service is free. Place the tool with emergency supplies and have another by the main or with a neighbor.

Locate the circuit breaker main or fuse box. Have family helpers assist in checking that all circuits are correctly labeled and in good working order. Learn how to turn the main power off by flicking the switches in the box to the off position. Replace bad fuses. Be sure to stock spare fuses to use in case of outages. As usage of electricity increases in the home through the addition of multi-outlet plugs and small appliances, stereos, etc., fuse boxes may need to be upgraded to breaker boxes. If anything appears to be loose or sparking, or if power outages or irregularities are occurring, call a licensed electrician to have it looked at. Have this safety check include a written estimate for any work or upgrading that needs to be done. If nothing is obviously wrong but you want to learn the system, call your electrical company with any questions and have a trained representative come to your home to show you how to work and maintain the system.

Locate the gas shutoff valve and tool, and check it to make sure it operates without getting stuck. In a disaster, it will be important to know how to shutoff the valve at the meter if you smell gas. This could save your life by preventing an explosion. Turn the valve 1/4 turn clockwise. Do not turn the gas back on yourself or relight the pilot light. Call the gas company to send a technician to turn the gas back on and relight the pilot light.

5. STRUCTURAL SUPPORT

The wood frame home is the most common type of dwelling. These structures are considered safe and flexible. The key in an earth movement type disaster or a big storm or flood is to make sure your home behaves as one unit, flexing, but not to the point of breaking either the supports or their connections. The aim is to distribute the force evenly throughout the house.

6. FOUNDATION

If your home was built after 1950 in the United States, the frame must have been bolted to the foundation to have met the building code. Before 1950 foundation bolting was not required. To ensure the continuity and longevity of your structure, make sure your home's foundation is bolted down. Contact a professional, either a licensed contractor or a seismic retrofitter in your area for someone qualified to do this kind of work. When dealing with contractors, always be sure to ask for references, contractor board certification numbers, and insurance information, including liability limits and bonding company. Always get a written estimate in advance of any work detailing costs, deposits, and timelines. Have labor and material costs separated.

You can do retrofitting yourself, but be aware that bolting floor joists directly to the foundation of your home is hard work done in small crawl spaces with heavy hand-held power tools and proper protective equipment.

Do-it-yourselfers can retrofit their own homes for less than a third of the cost a contractor will charge. While this not an easy job, experts say that it can be done by the home owner. Be sure to apply for any required building permits before you begin the work. The cost of retrofitting your home, whether you hire someone else to do it or not, will be far less than the potential catastrophic damage and danger of an unsecured dwelling.

7. SHEATHING

In the 1989 San Francisco World Series quake, many structures that failed to hold up were of the "soft story" type. Garages with exposed studs are a prime example of a "soft story" structure if the garage space supports living space above it. Garages can be sheathed with 1/2 inch plywood to strengthen the structure. It is possible to support the header beam and the garage door opening with plywood. Sheathing should be done in any area where remodeling has occurred and around picture windows. For professional advice call a licensed structural engineer to determine the adequacy of existing plywood siding in your home. Do what is needed to meet current building codes, including seeing that required permits are in order and posted.

8. BOLTING

A visit to your local building supply dealer will educate you to the numerous metal connectors available to secure any joint in your home. Anchor porches and decks to the main house. Secure plumbing lines and gas lines every few feet with straps connected to walls, ceilings, or floor joists.

INTERIOR HAZARDS

Use the following room inventory to identify the danger points and secure items that could be hazardous or sustain damage.

1. LIVING ROOM

The living room is where company is hosted and it is where you put your best foot forward. Collectibles, art, and antiques reside here, along with some of the heaviest pieces of furniture in your home. Safeguard your valuables and bolt down the top-heavy items.

- Secure pictures—close hooks, screw frames to wall studs.

- Safety-film sky lights, windows, sliders, French doors.

- Secure and safety-film mirrors.

- Secure artwork—close hooks, screw frames to wall studs.

- Bracket bookshelves to wall studs.

- Bracket TV, VCR, and stereo or stick with Velcro.

- Bolt large furniture to the wall studs or to the floor.

- Weight vases, ceramics, and sculptures with bean bags.

- Putty-fasten collectibles to shelves.

- Move heavy items to lower shelves.

2. KITCHEN

This is the most dangerous room in the house. Dishes, glasses, pots, and pans may fly missile-like out of cabinets and shelves. The refrigerator and stove may spring free and bulldoze anything in their paths. Exploding gas appliances can torch the house and injure its occupants. Have a healthy respect for these hazards and stay away from the kitchen in any disaster. Following is a list of steps to take in making the kitchen safer and more secure.

- Brace or block the refrigerator.

- Safety-film skylights, windows, sliders, and French doors.

- Secure the dishwasher.

- Install nonskid padding on shelves.

- Install child-security drawer and cabinet guards.

- Protect plates, bowls, and cups with foam sleeves.

- Protect glasses and wine bottles in styrofoam containers or compartments with cardboard dividers, as in wine cases.

- Pack heirloom china, crystal, and other such valuables in newspaper in boxes and store in a secure place.

- Install flexhose on gas appliances.

3. FAMILY ROOM

This is a multipurpose room with heavy traffic. The family gathers here on a daily basis. Be aware of all glass in the room and tall, heavy furniture such as entertainment centers and bookshelves when making preparations. Following is a list of steps to take in making the family room safer and more secure:

- Move heavy objects to lower shelves.

- Secure pictures—close hooks, screw frames to wall studs.

- Apply safety film to glass, skylights, sliders.

- Secure artwork, photographs.

- Bracket bookshelves to wall studs.

- Anchor entertainment center to wall studs.

- Bracket TV, VCR, stereo or stick with Velcro.

- Bolt large furniture to the floor.

- Weight vases, ceramics and sculptures with bean bags.

- Putty-fasten collectibles to shelves.

4. DINING ROOM

As increasingly, families live in their kitchens and family rooms, the dining room is often designated for more formal gatherings. If possible, close off this room when not in use. Following is a list of steps to take in making the dining room safer and more secure.

- Brace chandelier.

- Secure mirrors—close hooks, screw frame to wall studs.

- Bracket side tables, buffets, hutches.

- Remove casters from any large pieces of furniture, tables.

- Install nonskid padding where serving dishes, silver, and crystal are kept.

- Install child-security drawer and cabinet guards.

- Putty-fasten vases and candlesticks.

- Anchor buffet, highboy, hutches, and side tables to wall studs.

- Safety-film glass and windows.

- Move heavy objects to lower shelves.

5. BATHROOM

Bathrooms are full of glass. Mirrors, windows, skylights, shower doors, and glass containers abound. If cleaning supplies are kept in the bathroom, there are possible chemical spills to contend with in a disaster. You may want to use plastic containers as much as possible. Following is a list of steps to take in making the bathroom safer and more secure:

- Secure hanging plants.

- Safety-film glass, mirrors, windows, and skylights.

- Install child-security drawer and cabinet guards.

- Secure pictures—close hooks.

- Store shampoos, razors, and breakables in drawers.

- Eliminate glass containers or replace with plastic.

- Move heavy objects to lower shelves.

6. BEDROOM

The bedroom is your resting place at night. Eliminate hazards that could fall on you such as mirrors and framed art. Stabilize the bed with carpeting, removable casters, or wooden blocks to prevent the bed from moving. Secure or eliminate heavy furniture. Following is a list of steps to take in making the bedroom safer and more secure:

- Secure pictures–close hooks and screw frames to wall studs.

- Secure and safety-film mirrors.

- Safety-film windows, skylights.

- As an alternative to safety film, draw drapes or Venetian blinds overnight.

- Bolt dressers, armoires, and desks to wall studs.

- Install child security drawers and cabinet guards.

- Remove casters from beds or block legs.

- Attach bunk beds, bracket to wall studs.

- Bracket TV, VCR, stereo or fasten with Velcro.

- Bracket bookshelves together and to wall studs.

- Move heavy objects to lower shelves.

7. OFFICE/DEN

The office or den is a catchall room for the whole family with numerous functions, from reading and working on the computer to watching TV. Following is a list of steps to take in making the office or den safer and more secure:

- Remove casters from furniture.

- Bracket bookshelves to wall studs.

- Secure file cabinet drawers.

- Bracket TV, VCR, stereo equipment.

- Secure computer, printer, accessories.

- Store computer external hard drive on the floor.

- Secure exercise equipment.

- Apply safety film to windows, mirrors.

8. GARAGE/LAUNDRY

The garage and laundry rooms receive almost as much use as the kitchen. Many odds and ends and heavier equipment are relegated to these locations. Store all items carefully. Always handle toxic substances with extreme caution as they can emit lethal fumes or even explode when disturbed.

- Place firewood in heavy boxes bolted to floor.

- Store toxics and flammables, such as house paint, cleaning chemicals, motor oil, propane camp stoves,and gasoline cans in boxes secured to floor.

- Use child-security drawer and cabinet latches.

- Secure tools in containers that latch.

- Tie building materials with bungee cords.

- Secure propane tanks. In case of flooding, these can become floating bombs.

- Move heavy objects to lower shelves.

- Secure refrigerator or freezer doors.

- Use flexible hoses for gas clothes dryer.

- Secure hot water heater with plumber's tape or bolt in place.

9. SUPPLIES STORAGE

You will need to gather food and store water. Check the kitchen pantry for foods that will keep in storage, such as canned goods. Include food that you like to eat to make survival more bearable. Food from the refrigerator can be eaten, freshest food first, frozen foods last, over a period of 4-7 days. Replace foods annually. Store water in plastic, nonbreakable jugs or buy bottled water. Allow one gallon per person per day, 1/2 gallon for drinking (more if you live in a hot, dry climate) and 1/2 gallon for washing. Also store water for pets. If you are storing water in recycled containers, clean quart or liter plastic pop containers thoroughly. Label each bottle with the fill date and refill every six months to keep the supply of water fresh. Do not refill empty milk, detergent, or bleach bottles as toxic effects may result.

Other supplies to gather are personal health and hygiene articles, camping equipment, tools, pet supplies, and first aid items. Your camping equipment may be your best immediate source of shelter after the disaster and it may allow you to stay on your own property and monitor the situation. Include any special prescription medications in your first aid kit and be sure to discard outdated prescriptions once a year. When old supplies are discarded, they should be replaced.

Decide where you are going to store emergency supplies, including the Red Cross First Aid Manual, and put everything in one place. It is best to pick a cool, dark place that will be safe and accessible. A garage, a closet, part of the basement, or under a bed are all good places. This is also a good time to collect supplies for the office and the childrens' school or daycare and distribute them accordingly. Automobiles should have emergency kits placed in the trunk.

For evacuation, you need supply containers that are easy to move. Back packs, coolers, and large garbage cans with wheels and clamp-down lids work well.

HEALTH AND HYGIENE LIST

You will want the following ordinary daily cleaning aids packed with your emergency supplies. Work from the following suggested list.

- Toothbrush, toothpaste, floss

- Shampoo, lotion

- Comb, brush, mirror

- Bar soap, washcloth

- Shaving kit, deodorant

- Baby wipes, cream, diapers

- Toilet paper

- Plastic dishpan

- Towel(s)

- Sanitary pads, tampons

- Chlorinated lime powder (latrine disinfectant)

- Eyedropper, eyewash

- Large plastic garbage bags and ties

- Plastic bucket (portable toilet)

- Liquid bleach (5.25 sodium hypochlorite)

- One-half gallon of washing water per day, per person

CAMPING EQUIPMENT LIST

In a disaster, temporary shelter or sleeping and eating facilities may not be available. In any event, a suggested list of camping supplies should be stored for your comfort. Work from the following suggested list:

- Foil space blankets

- Wool blankets

- Tent, sleeping bags

- Three tarps (one under tent, one over supplies, one over tent)

- Multifunction camping knife

- Mess kits or plastic plates, cups, bowls and utensils

- Manual can opener, Swiss army knife

- Ice chest

- Ax, shovel

- Fluorescent or battery-powered lantern

- Flashlight and separate alkaline batteries

- Portable radio or TV

- Bungee cords, 50'-75' Nylon cord, rope

- Local map

- Postcards, pens, stamps, books and periodicals

- Bucket of sand (stove and fireplace fires)

- ABC fire extinguisher

- Pepper spray or mace

- Clock (nonelectric)

- Toys, games

TOOLS AND MATERIALS LIST

You will need tools and materials to dislodge rubble and make necessary repairs. Work from the following suggested list:

- Second-story length ladder

- Axe

- Rake

- Long-handled, round-point shovel

- Chainsaw

- Hammer

- Nails and screws

- Set of crescent wrenches or adjustable wrench

- Pliers

- Phillips screwdriver

- Flat-end screwdriver

- Large staple gun and staples

- Electrician's tape

- Heavy-duty, cloth duct tape

- Plastic sheeting

- Sandbags

- Plywood

- Boards

- Water-main wrench

- Gas-main wrench

- Crowbar

FOOD LIST

Storage of food and water is essential for survival. Choose foods that will not spoil and foods that your family will enjoy. It will be very important psychologically to have something good to eat in the midst of chaos and transition. Food and water should be rotated and replaced annually. The following list may be stored in case of disaster.

- Freeze dried meals, dried fruit

- Nuts, granola bars

- Canned salmon, sardines, oysters, clams, and tuna

- Canned soup, chili, beans, stew

- Crackers, cookies

- Cereal, oatmeal

- Peanut butter

- Powdered or canned milk

- Baby food

- Cans of vegetable or fruit juice

- Canned Spam or deviled ham

- Canned cheese

- Pet food

- One-half gallon of drinking water per day per person or pet. (minimum allotment = 3 days use)

FIRST AID LIST

First aid kits may be purchased from the Red Cross, your local pharmacy, or a camping supply store. You can gather many items from your own medicine chest or camping supplies. Work from the following suggested list.

- Red Cross First Aid Manual

- Sterile surgical gloves

- Aspirin or Non-aspirin

- Rubbing alcohol

- Hydrogen peroxide, boric acid

- Campho-Phenique, iodine

- Cortisone creme, vaseline

- Insect repellent, golden seal ointment

- Calamine lotion

- Sterile cotton balls, Q-Tips, eyedropper

- Assorted sterile gauze bandages and tape

- Triangle, ace, and butterfly bandages

- Scissors, tweezers

- Thread, needle, safety pins

- Vitamins, homeopathic remedies, current prescriptions

- Safety goggles, backup prescription eyeglasses

- Pocket mask with disposable mouth valve

- Medical release forms, physicians' directives, power of attorney forms

PET SUPPLY LIST

Here is a list of items to store for your pets. Your veterinarian may have additional recommendations. Work from the following suggested list:

- Pet carriers, leashes, and litter boxes

- Sand or pet litter

- Pet food and water, 1/2 gallon per day for drinking, three-day supply

- Pet prescriptions

- Manual can opener

- Bowls, water pails, plastic bags, towel, blanket, brush

- Disinfectants, flea powder

- Hydrogen peroxide (cuts, wounds, poisonings)

- Betadine solution (non-stinging iodine)

- Neosporin antibiotic ointment

- Diarrhea medication

- Constipation medication

- Rectal thermometer

- Vaseline

- Bandages and tape

PERSONAL BUSINESS LIST

You will want to have important information on hand in order to expedite your personal affairs, including insurance data and your out-of-the-area contact person. For example:

- Cash ($500.00 per family recommended), change for pay phone

- Insurance policy

- Appraisals

- Fireproof strongbox (as carrier)

- Photos (house, improvements, family)

- Contact person information

- Emergency information

- Identification, birth certificates

- Family medical information

- Video tape of personal possessions

- Car key, house key, safe deposit key

CAR LIST

When you are traveling to and from work or on short trips or vacations you will need to be equipped to deal with a sudden event. Always have seasonal gear for changing weather conditions and the possibility of being stranded in your car waiting for help from rescue crews. Keep the suggested items in the trunk of your car and glove box:

- At least 1/2 a tank of gasoline

- First Aid Kit

- Two or three gallons of water (leave 2" at top in case of freezing)

- Flares

- Flashlight, separate alkaline batteries

- Portable radio, separate alkaline batteries

- Map, extra glasses, identification, medical alert tags

- Dry matches in dry, airtight container

- Portable shovel

- ABC fire extinguisher

- Heavy work gloves, shoes, warm clothing

- Raingear, umbrella

- Tarp, blankets (wool, solar), bright signal cloth

- Bungee cords

- Canned food, nuts, juices, manual can opener, utensils, cup

- Tire chains, towing rope

- Battery cables

- Help sign

- Window scraper

- Contact person information

- Emergency information

- Sandbag

- Cash, change for pay phone

OFFICE LIST

Plan on being stranded at the office for three days and allow sufficient supplies for that time frame. Services may be cut off in the event of a disaster and roads may not be accessible. You may need the following:

- Three gallons water

- Cash, change for pay phone, identification

- Personal hygiene items—toothbrush, hairbrush, shampoo

- Emergency information

- Contact person information

- Flashlight, separate alkaline batteries

- Portable radio, separate alkaline batteries

- Canned food, nuts, juice, manual can opener, utensils, cup

- Raingear, warm clothing, heavy gloves, and shoes

- First Aid Kit, medications

- Sleeping bag, mat

SHOPPING LIST

You will not be able to find every item in one place.

WHAT TO BUY	WHERE TO BUY
• No-slip foam shelving	R.V. store
• Cabinet/drawer guards	hardware store
• Plumbers tape	hardware store
• Putty, wood screws	hardware store
• Lag bolts/molly bolts	hardware store
• Picture hangers	hardware store
• L brackets/T straps	hardware store
• Plywood	lumber yard
• Foam sleeves for china	packaging store
• Cardboard boxes/dividers	packaging store
• Styrofoam bottle protectors	packaging store

- Pocket mask   Red Cross

- First-aid manual and kit   Red Cross

- Stereo brackets   Stereo store

EARTHQUAKES

Earthquakes have struck without warning in every season all over the world. Devastating quakes have rocked China, France, Portugal, Chile, Japan, and the United States, most recently in Hawaii, Oregon, and California. Earthquakes are raging events which can cause enormous damage in a minute or less. The San Francisco "World Series" quake of 1989 lasted ten seconds and did ten billion dollars of damage.

An earthquake is defined as a series of elastic waves in the crust of the earth, caused by a sudden relaxation of strains accumulated along geologic faults and by volcanic action, and with resulting movements in the earth's crust. An earthquake is the most dramatic and far-reaching of disasters with its roaring freight train noise, shaking ground, and tremendous power. The destruction is particularly great when the earthquake hits an urban area where buildings collapse and freeways twist and/or fracture. When gas lines explode, fires frequently follow. Tsunamis may occur as a result of the earthquake and devastate coastal areas. Floods, volcanic eruptions, and landslides can also follow or occur simultaneously.

Preparation for an earthquake includes getting insurance information and coverage, documenting your possessions, receiving first aid training, holding family and neighborhood meetings, storing of supplies, choosing an out-of-the-area contact person, retrofitting your home, securing hazards inside, and having evacuation and return procedures.

BEFORE THE QUAKE

OUTSIDE

- Check powerline locations for areas to avoid after the quake.

- Remove tree limbs that might ignite on shorting power lines.

- Have an arborist remove trees that might fall on the house.

- Brace chimneys.

- Brace ceiling joists by chimney with plywood.

- Bolt floor joists to the foundation.

- Bolt stories together, reinforce joints.

- Sheath garage with exposed studs with 1/2" plywood.

- Sheath any remodeled area.

- Sheath around picture windows.

- Anchor porches and decks to the main house.

- Meet with structural engineer to check adequacy of plywood siding.

- Upgrade to meet current building codes as necessary.

- Call a seismic retrofitter or licensed building contractor to do the bracing and bolting if you are unable to do it yourself.

- Check fuse box or circuit breaker. Replace bad fuses and stock spares. Upgrade fuse boxes using a licensed electrician if necessary

- Practice turning off water at the main in the street.

- Check gas meter, place tool nearby—in emergency kit, with a neighbor.

INSIDE

- Get insurance and document your possessions.

- Take first aid, CPR class.

- Bolt water heater to wall.

- Secure plumbing and gas lines every few feet with straps connected to walls, ceilings, or floor joists.

- Put flexible hoses on gas appliances.

- Secure interior room by room.

- Store food, water, and other supplies.

- Attend community and neighborhood meetings.

DURING THE QUAKE

- If walking outdoors, stay outdoors.

- Avoid trees, powerlines, tall buildings, and overpasses.

- Look for an open meadow and go there.

- If you are driving your car over a bridge or an overpass calmly drive off and pull over.

- If power lines fall across your car, roll up the windows and stay in the car.

- If you are at the coast or next to a bay, lake, or river head for the high ground as fast as you can.

- Pay attention to tsunami warnings and sirens. Do not go toward the ocean to see what is happening.

• If you are in bed, roll off the bed onto the floor, and stay next to the bed.

• Do not try to contain pets or rescue others. Wait until the movement stops before moving elsewhere.

• If you are in the house, move away from glass, brick, mirrors, and large pieces of furniture.

• Get under a desk or table and stay there until the quake is over.

• If you are in a wheelchair, stay in your chair.

• Move your wheelchair next to an interior wall away from windows and falling objects. Set the brake and cover your head.

• If you are in a crowd in a movie theatre or an opera house, do not panic. Duck, cover, and hold on.

• Do not leave your seat until the movement stops, then use emergency exits as directed.

• If you are in a building do not use the elevators.

• If you are working in your office, stay there. Take cover under your desk, next to an interior wall or in a doorway away from windows and masonry.

AFTER THE QUAKE

• Put heavy shoes and clothes on everyone

• Assist others and render first aid as safety permits.

• Tune into radio reports for confirmed information.

• If you are not home, know road damage
  conditions and emergency routes before
  attempting to drive home.

• Go to the family's prearranged meeting spot

• Check the outside of the house for chimney
  damage, separation of exterior walls, attachments,
  porches, decks.

• Do not go inside the house if it appears at all
  unstable.

• Do not go in the house if the ground is shifting.
  Evacuate.

• Leave the house in case of landslides.

• Do not go in places where the roof or walls have
  collapsed.

- Put out small fires with fire extinguisher or evacuate the house.

- Do not light a match.

- Check for gas leaks.

- If a gas smell is detected, turn gas off at the meter (1/4 turn clockwise). Evacuate if smell continues.

- Turn off water main at the street.

- Check for loose or broken wires or shorts. Do not touch.

- Shut off electricity off at circuit breaker box.

- Use drain plugs in tubs, showers, and sinks to prevent sewer backup.

- Do not use toilets, sewers may be blocked.

• Ventilate. Open doors and windows.

• Turn off all appliances.

• Do not turn the gas back on yourself. Call the gas company to relight pilot.

• Put phones back on hooks. Do not use the phone except for 911 emergencies.

• Check furnace, evacuate if ducts or pipes are torn exposing asbestos.

• Stay tuned to the radio for news and instructions.

• Clean up toxic spills, inflammables, glass.

• Clear fallen bricks from paths and roof.

• Evacuate in case of flooding.

- Thaw refrigerator ice cubes for drinking water.

- Use non-chemically treated toilet tank (not bowl) or hot water heater as emergency water sources.

- Purify collected emergency water with bleach.

- Do not eat food found near broken glass.

- Tie a red, white, or yellow signal ribbon to your front door.

- Go to pay phone and report to contact person.

- Leave the house in case of tsunami warnings.

- Prepare for aftershocks. Take down unsecured pictures and artwork.

- Leave fallen objects down.

- Wrap breakables in blankets.

• Open cabinets and closets carefully, be careful of broken and falling objects and dishes.

• Fasten cabinet knobs.

• Use duct tape and plastic to mend cracked windows.

• Use plywood to board up broken windows.

HURRICANES

The turbulent storms known as hurricanes arise in the tropical regions of the Caribbean Sea and Atlantic Ocean. In the United States, more hurricanes occur near Florida than in any other state. The storms take place from late June through December, and are most active in August and September. The Caribbean Islands, the West Indies, the Canary Islands, and the Gulf of Mexico are persistently areas plagued by hurricanes.

Hurricanes are members of the family of storms called tropical cyclones, which includes their cousins, cyclones and typhoons. A hurricane is a spectacular, rotary storm of 300 to 400 miles in diameter, that swirls around a calm center. Its rains and winds drive at speeds of 75 miles per hour and greater. These storms can become extremely dangerous. The crushing winds of up to 200 miles per hour may exert more than a ton of pressure on each 10 square feet of the open face of a building.

The migration patterns of hurricanes are northerly, veering slightly both to the west and east from their points of origin. In one observation, "A hurricane formed off the coast of Africa might trample the West Indies, take a swipe at Cuba or the Bahamas–then tear into the American mainland from the Gulf of Mexico or Florida." Violent downpours and nearly horizontal rains can spawn severe flooding, the waters rising from 5 inches to 15 inches in a few hours. Hurricanes also spur storm surges, tidal waves, and landslides, destroying property and eroding beachfronts.

Preparation for a hurricane will include getting insurance, documenting possessions and property, checking and restocking stored supplies each June before the prime time of arrival and again before the end of the season in December. Taking a first aid class, attending community meetings, securing the house, building a shelter or designating a safe place to ride out the storm, and listening to the radio for storm advisories and evacuation instructions will also be useful.

BEFORE THE HURRICANE

If you hear the first tropical storm advisory you will be able to plan your strategy and movements in advance. Stay tuned for a hurricane watch, meaning possible danger within 24 hours; and plan your time so that you are not caught outside with the possibility of being caught or marooned when the storm breaks.

OUTSIDE

• Fill your car's gas tank with gas.

• Watch the weather, look for darkening skies, rising wind, and rain torrents. Stay alert.

• Secure or take inside garbage cans, lawn furniture, gardening tools, barbecues, children's toys, or any object that could be hurled by the wind.

• If at the beach, watch for waves coming inland.

• Leave low-lying areas due to danger from high tides and flooding.

• If swimming or in a boat, get to shore and seek shelter.

• Secure the boat or evacuate it to a pre-designated safe area.

• Check your portable radio for news and instructions.

- Board up windows, close shutters, or tape glass. Wind pressure can shatter large windows and flying debris can break smaller panes of glass.

- Contain pets and livestock.

INSIDE

- Get insurance and document your possessions.

- Take First Aid and CPR classes.

- Attend community Civil Defense meetings.

- Secure your home room by room.

- Listen for storm advisories and warnings on the radio or TV.

- Check your supplies, camping equipment, and emergency cooking equipment.

• Move valuables and your family to the side of the house away from the wind.

• Check flashlights and portable radio for fresh batteries.

• Store water before the supply can be contaminated. Plastic bottles, clean jugs, pots and pans and even the bathtub can serve as receptacles.

• If you are in a mobile home or an R.V. Park, leave the premises when you hear the storm warning and go to a designated shelter.

• Monitor the storm by listening to the radio or TV. Evacuate according to instructions.

• Contain pets by leash or carrier.

DURING THE HURRICANE

• If your home is on high ground and solidly built, stay in and wait out the storm.

• Do not try to rescue pets or people during the storm.

• Beware of the eye, the calm center of the storm, as it passes overhead. The calm can last from two minutes to half an hour.

• If you have a basement or storm cellar, that is the place to wait out the storm.

• If you do not have a basement, go to the lowest floor of your home, away from windows or any thing that could hurt you.

• If you are in a wheelchair, set the brake and cover your head.

• If at work, or in a public building, follow procedures. Get away from glass.

• If walking outside, take cover immediately, get down.

• If driving, park the car, get out, and seek cover under a freeway overpass, doorway, or stairwell.

• Avoid power lines, trees, buildings and windows.

• If possible, stay calm.

AFTER THE HURRICANE

• Check for injuries and render first aid.

• Put heavy shoes and clothes on everyone.

- Avoid driving if possible. If driving is necessary, drive with caution. Debris may be hazardous and roads can collapse if undermined. Landslides are also possible.

- Stay away from river banks and streams.

- Listen to your radio for information such as flood warnings, location of shelters, road damage, Red Cross stations, and emergency routes.

- Go to Red Cross disaster stations for emergency medical attention.

- Stay away from disaster areas unless qualified to help. First aid and rescue workers will function best unhampered.

- Beware of loose or dangling electrical wires. Report to police or power company.

- If separated from your family, use contact person.

• Report broken sewers and water mains to your utility company.

• Use caution when returning home or to pre-arranged family meeting spot.

• Do not go into the house if it looks unstable.

• Check for gas leaks. Do not light a match.

• Clean up toxic spills as possible.

• Put phones on hooks. Do not use except for 911 emergency.

• Check the outside of the house for damage to chimneys, wall cracks, and porch and deck stairways.

• Stay away from river banks and streams where flooding can occur. Hurricanes moving inland can bring severe flooding.

- See floods section for what steps to take in case of a flood.

- Keep animals contained for awhile.

- Evacuate if directed by authorities.

TORNADOS

Tornados embattle Europe, Asia, North America, West Africa, and the nearby Atlantic. The central and Southeast area of the United States is the tornado hot spot of the world, known as Tornado Alley, where these whirling storms rack up a toll of approximately 700 events a year. The states targeted the most are Texas, Arkansas, Oklahoma, Kansas, Nebraska, and Missouri. Late winter in the southern United States is the time to watch and, as the storms charge at full tilt northward, they reach into Canada's prairie provinces in June, July, and August.

A tornado is a column of air rotating under the funnel-shaped bottom of a cumulo-nimbus cloud. These so-called 'twisters' can be generated in the updraft of a thunderstorm or a hurricane moving overhead. Broad as several hundred yards in diameter, the tornado's cork-screw winds fly at speeds of up to 300 miles per hour on a path about half a mile wide. Under dark yellow skies, the powerful vacuum in the storm's funnel is capable of seizing up, hoisting, and exploding a house in its wake. The grinding roar of the tornado has been compared to a jet plane taking off, the noise results from the friction of the high winds as they chafe against the ground. When condensation does not develop in the storm, its shadowy silhouette may only be delineated by the dust and debris it carries aloft over the land. If a tornado sucks up water spray over the ocean, this is called a waterspout, and these are most frequently sighted on the Florida coast and in the Bahamas.

Preparation for a tornado will include obtaining insurance and documenting possessions and property, storing supplies, creating a basement space or cyclone shelter or knowing the location of a nearby emergency shelter, watching the weather forecasts, and staying alert to changing weather conditions and warnings.

BEFORE THE TORNADO

OUTSIDE

- Fill your car's gas tank with gas.

- Watch the weather, look for darkening skies, rising wind, and rain torrents. Stay alert.

- If at the beach, watch for waves coming inland.

- Leave low-lying areas due to danger from high tides and flooding.

- Check your portable radio for news and instructions.

- If swimming or in a boat, get to shore and seek shelter. Secure the boat or evacuate it to a pre-designated safe area.

• Secure or take inside garbage cans, lawn
  furniture, gardening tools, barbecues, children's
  toys, or any object that could be hurled by the
  wind.

• Board up windows, close shutters, or tape glass.
  Wind pressure can shatter large windows and
  flying debris can break smaller panes of glass.

• Contain pets and livestock.

INSIDE

• Get insurance and document your possessions.

• Attend community Civil Defense meetings.

• Take First Aid and CPR classes.

• Secure your home.

• Listen for storm advisories and warnings on the radio or TV.

• Check your supplies, camping equipment and emergency cooking equipment.

• Move valuables and your family to the side of the house away from the wind.

• Check flashlights and portable radio, use fresh batteries.

• Store water before the supply can be contaminated. Plastic bottles, clean jugs, pots and pans, and even the bathtub can serve as receptacles.

• If you are in a mobile home or R.V. Park, leave the premises when you hear the storm warning and go to a designated shelter.

• Monitor the storm by listening to the radio or TV.

• Prepare to evacuate according to instructions.

DURING THE TORNADO

• If you have a storm cellar, wait out the storm there.

• If caught by the storm while outside, move away from its path at a right angle.

• If walking outside, duck into a stairwell or cul-
vert.

• If in a building with a freestanding roof such as an
auditorium or gymnasium, seek other shelter.

• If there is no time to escape, drop to the ground in
the nearest ditch, ravine, or depression.

• Remain calm during the storm and stay put.

• If your home is on high ground and sturdy, stay in
and wait out the storm.

• Beware of the eye, the calm center of the storm,
as it passes overhead. The calm lasts from two
minutes to half an hour.

• If you do not have a basement, go to the lowest
floor of your home, away from windows or glass
doors.

• In a factory or warehouse, avoid walls and windows, go to a predetermined safe area.

• Get away from upper floors and open areas and go to interior hallways, reinforced rooms, or partitioned basement space.

• If your basement is unpartitioned, go to the center or under a stairwell.

• Contain pets by leash or carrier.

• If you are outside, get inside quickly.

• If you are in a car, seek shelter immediately, even in a ditch.

AFTER THE TORNADO

• Check for injuries and render first aid.

• Avoid driving if possible.

• If driving is necessary, drive with caution. Debris may be hazardous and roads can collapse if undermined. Landslides are also possible.

• Listen to your radio for information such as flood warnings and location of shelters and Red Cross stations.

• Go to Red Cross disaster stations for emergency medical attention.

• Stay away from disaster areas unless qualified to help. First aid and rescue workers will function best unhampered.

- Beware of loose or dangling electrical wires. Report to police or power company.

- Report broken sewers and water mains to your utility company.

- Stay away from river banks and streams where flooding can occur. Hurricanes moving inland frequently bring severe flooding.

- Approach animals and pets with caution.

- Keep animals contained.

- Put heavy shoes and clothes on everyone.

- Use caution when returning home or to pre-arranged family meeting spot.

- Do not go into the house if it looks unstable.

• If separated from your family, use contact person.

• Check for gas leaks. Do not light a match.

• Clean up toxic spills as possible.

• Put phones on hooks. Do not use except for 911 emergency.

• Check the outside of the house for damage to chimneys, wall cracks, and porch and deck stairways.

FLOODS

Floods can occur anywhere on the globe following several hours to several days of intense or prolonged rainfall which forces streams or rivers to overflow their banks. A flood is defined as a deluge of water overtaking, covering, and submerging normally dry land. When a natural, seasonal rise in temperature produces the spring thaw, this melting of winter's accumulation of snow occasionally unleashes flooding. If a dam or levee bursts, flash flooding can amplify rapidly, in just a few minutes or a few hours. A number of disasters can precipitate floods, including earthquakes, tsunamis, hurricanes, and other volatile wind and rain storms. Tidal waves propelled by the turbulence of hurricanes may perpetuate floods, dumping giant cisterns of seawater on shore, sopping up vast spans of coastline land.

Preparation for a flood will include getting flood insurance, documenting possessions, taking first aid classes, attending community meetings on evacuation procedures, and storing supplies.

BEFORE THE FLOOD

• Take First Aid and CPR classes.

• Attend community meetings.

• Contact local emergency authorities and find out if your home is on the flood plain.

• Do not build on the flood plain.

• Contact your insurance agent for flood insurance and document your possessions.

- Contact the National Flood Insurance Program to see if your community qualifies for insurance.

- Get information on what to do in case of flooding even if not at risk at home-in case you may be vacationing or visiting when a flood occurs.

- Fill the bathtub with drinking water before supply is contaminated.

- Store emergency supplies including rubber boots and gloves.

- Store sandbags, plywood, plastic sheeting and lumber to be used in battening the hatches against flood waters.

- Store combustible toxic materials such as propane tanks, spray paint, gasoline cans, motor oil, and propane camp stoves.

• Plan evacuation procedures, including items to take
  and destination in unendangered area such as
  motel, friend's home, or shelter.

• Get several maps and designate two or three
  alternate routes to your destination in different
  color, permanent felt-tip markers.

• Store one map in the car and one in the
  emergency supply kit.

• Plan for flood warnings by learning the
  terminology.

• Watch news and listen to the radio for forecasts
  and instructions.

• Fill your car's gas tank.

DURING THE FLOOD

- If the term " flood forecast" is broadcast, be aware that heavy rains may cause rivers to overflow.

- If the term "flood warning" is broadcast, be aware that flooding is now occurring or will occur soon.

- If the term "flash flood warning" is broadcast, areas will be specified where sudden floods are expected or occurring.

- Turn off the utilities.

- Prepare to follow evacuation procedures.

- Evacuate immediately to higher ground.

- If driving, avoid storm drains and irrigation ditches.

- Never drive around a police blockade.

- Listen to the radio for instructions on what to do.

- If water is rising around your car and the car won't start, abandon your vehicle at once and get to higher ground.

- Place sandbags, secure your home as instructed.

- Do not wait to evacuate if you see a flood approaching.

AFTER THE FLOOD

- Check for injuries and apply first aid.

- Call 911 for help as necessary.

- Listen to radio for information and instruction.

- Wait for confirmed reports of improving conditions and safe routes home.

- Use caution in returning home.

- Avoid flood-damaged areas.

- Be cautious of pets and livestock, contain and comfort pets.

WILDFIRES

Wildfires break out all over the world, sparked by tinderbox, drought conditions prevalent in the summer and early fall. Conditions are optimum for spontaneous combustion that kindles these fires when the temperatures soar high and vegetation is without moisture. Strong winds can fan the flames over dry prairies and timberlands. Lightning bolts hurled by electrically-charged thunderstorms are often the flint that ignites forest fires. It is estimated that the damage in the U.S. alone is up to three billion dollars per year. Indirectly, some wildfires are caused by cyclones conveying thunderstorms and lightning. Shorts from downed power lines and from electrical lines leading to your home or exterior buildings can also spark a wildfire. Hot molten lava from volcanic eruptions sets vegetation in its path on fire as well.

Preparation for a wildfire will include getting fire insurance, documenting possessions and property, attending Red Cross first aid classes, attending community fire safety and evacuation meetings, safeguarding your home, having a water supply backup, storing supplies, and being aware of optimum weather conditions and fire warnings.

BEFORE THE WILDFIRE

OUTSIDE

- If building a house in a forested area, contact the forestry department for recommendations on materials to use.

- Use fire resistant materials when constructing a home, including treated wood products, stone, aluminum, and brick.

- Plant trees and bushes sparsely to avoid a path of fuel for the wildfire.

- Tear off wood shake roof and replace with noncombustible roof.

- Use asphalt rag-roll roofing, tile, slate, cement shingle, sheet metal, or aluminum roofing materials.

- Trim trees away from roofs of home and garage or shop.

- Plant large trees a minimum of ten feet away from your home's exterior.

- Generally landscape with low-growing plants.

- Always water and prune the landscaping well so that it can serve as a protective fireline.

- Store flammables away from the house.

• Check the power lines to keep tree branches clear and call the utility company if trees are touching the wires.

• Generally maintain tree and shrub pruning and trimming.

• Check to see that you are maintaining a 30 foot noncombustible, defensible space with no flammable vegetation in it all the way around your home to be a fire break.

• If you live on a hillside or by a forest, you will need additional clearing of up to 100 feet or more.

• Haul away yard debris before it starts to pile up.

• Clean gutters and roof regularly to remove combustible leaves and needles.

• Follow local burning restrictions and safety requirements when disposing of debris.

• Stack firewood away from the house, not going downhill (fires often travel uphill).

• Have an adequate water supply to fight a fire.

• Fill and test large water tanks (cisterns), stand pipes, fire hydrants, or wells with high volume pumps.

• Prepare to access swimming pools, ponds or storage tanks with portable pumps, check working condition of equipment.

• In case of electrical failure, have backup system (alternate power) for well pumps.

• Check water hoses to make sure they are long enough to reach all around the exterior of your home and test for leaks.

• Always keep a hose with a nozzle attachment connected to an outside outlet.

• Stock standard fire fighting tools such as an axe, a rake, a chainsaw, a long-handled, round-point shovel, and a 2 1/2 gallon water bucket.

• Have a ladder tall enough to reach your roof.

• Guarantee emergency and firetruck access by maintaining two way roads with parking lanes.

• Build roads that slope less than ten feet per 100 feet to make the going easier for cumbersome firetrucks that have trouble with steep roads.

• Clear the roadway of flammable brush and materials 60 feet wide along the right of way to prevent wildfire hazard.

INSIDE

- Get insurance and document your possessions.

- Attend community meetings on volcanos, earthquakes, and emergency evacuation procedures.

- Take Red Cross first aid, CPR and fire safety classes.

- Call a family meeting and discuss where to go, what to take, where to meet if separated, what to do about pets.

- Plan escape routes—one by foot and two by car.

- Know where you will go and what you will take in case of evacuation.

- Store emergency supplies, food and water.

- Post the number to call in case of fire by every phone.

- Install portable smoke detectors outside every sleeping area and on every level of your home and in garage and workshop.

- Use button to test smoke alarms twice a year.

- Store extra smoke alarm batteries.

- Keep fire extinguishers in the kitchen and hallways, test and replace immediately if faulty.

- Conduct fire drills, including walking or driving evacuation routes.

- Draw a floorplan and find two ways to escape from every room. Conduct drills.

- Get rope or chain ladders for upper stories and practice using.

DURING THE WILDFIRE

- Turn off gas at the meter to avoid danger of explosion.

- Put on heavy shoes and protective clothing.

- Take your stored supplies and complete evacuation procedures.

- Listen to radio for updates on the wildfire.

- Be sure to prepare to travel on a confirmed route.

- If stranded in a car, tie a bright cloth onto antenna and wait for rescue workers.

AFTER THE WILDFIRE

• Assist others and render first aid as safety permits.

• Listen to the radio reports for confirmed information and instructions including location of Red Cross Disaster Stations, shelters, and animal holding areas.

• Use caution going home. Do not return unless advised by authorities that conditions are safe and roads are clear.

• If driving is necessary, drive with caution.

• Avoid wildfire damaged and active areas.

• Go to Red Cross Disaster Station for emergency medical treatment.

• Check your home's exterior for damage and instability.

- Do not go inside if it appears unsafe.

- If other family members are not there, follow your plan for locating one another, including calling your out-of-the-area contact person.

- Approach animals with caution and comfort and contain as possible.

- Check and repair fenced areas for animals.

THUNDERSTORMS

Thunderstorms are the most prolific, common, and costly of storms. At any moment in time, 2,000 thunderstorms are deploying all over the globe, at 100 lightning strikes per second, and a cost of three billion dollars in damages. Every day there are 45,000 thunderstorms with an annual count of 16 million thunderstorms in the world. In the United States, where 100,000 of these thunderstorms rage every year, Florida is the most frequently assaulted state. Spring and summer are the prime times thunderstorms unleash, with afternoon and evening bringing the most action.

Generated from atmospheric temperature imbalances, these violent storms are caused by the upward transfer of heat known as convection. They can also arrive slip-streaming on the coattails of cyclones in flashing lightning, rumbling thunder, and pelting rain or hail with winds of up to 50 miles per hour. Flash flooding is a potential aftermath of such an outburst. Because thunderstorms come to life in massive, dark tents of cumulo-nimbus clouds which carry electric charges, they are electrical storms wielding potentially damaging lightning bolts. The roar of thunder is the sound of rapidly expanding gases in the path of the lightning's electrical discharge. Giant storms of 10 miles high can measure twice as wide. Separate, adjoining thunderstorms may spread out over several hundred miles to form what are known as squall lines. The storms, or cells, can continue by replacing old cells with new ones in relay fashion. Microbursts are quick, forceful surges that create hurricane-powerful, horizontal winds with speeds up to 200 miles per hour, tackling power lines, uprooting trees, shattering windows, damaging buildings, and blowing roofs off. Airplanes struck by sudden wind gusts and shifting vertical pressures have been known to crash due to their sustained structural damage.

Preparation for a thunderstorm will include getting property insurance and documenting possessions and property, taking a first aid and CPR class at the local Red Cross or YMCA, storing supplies, attending community meetings and learning flood safety and evacuation procedures and being aware of changing weather conditions including flash flood warnings.

BEFORE THE STORM

OUTSIDE

Be aware of warning signs, seen as changes in the weather. Lightning is the main danger of a thunderstorm. You are close enough to the storm to be struck by lightning if you can hear thunder. Seek shelter immediately.

• Look for darkening rain clouds and skies.

• Watch for light flashes.

• Be aware of increasing wind and lowering
  temperatures.

• Listen for thunder.

INSIDE

• Attend CPR and First Aid classes.

• Store supplies and water.

• Listen to news and watch weather forecasts and
  updates.

• Be aware of any flood warnings or watches.

• If a flood is predicted raise furniture and belongings off ground floor level.

DURING THE STORM

OUTSIDE

There are a number of safety precautions to take to
avoid being struck by lightning.

• Take cover in a building or a car (other than a
convertible) and close the windows.

• In the woods get under the shorter trees.

• In the water, swimming or in a boat, get to land
and look for shelter.

* Listen to portable radio for news and instruction.

• Go to a flat, open place where it will not be flooded.

• Keep away from trees, metal objects, or poles.

• Squat low to the ground, tuck head in between knees and put hands on knees. Make a small target. Do not lie flat on the ground.

• Get pets, livestock contained, put dogs on a leash, cats in a carrier.

INSIDE

Take precautions to avoid coming in contact with electricity which can be conducted through phone lines and metal pipes.

• Do not use the phone.

- Unplug appliances.

- Listen to battery-powered radio for storm news.

- Do not run water, bathe, or shower.

- Turn off air conditioning. Compressor units can be damaged by power surges.

- Draw shades and blinds to avoid shattering glass from windows as forceful winds blow objects into windows.

AFTER THE STORM

- Check for injuries and apply first aid.

- Call 911 for help if necessary.

• Aid lightning victims (Persons struck by lightning
  do not retain an electrical charge). Check for burns
  at entry and exit sites and treat accordingly. Give
  CPR if heart is stopped. Use mouth-to-mouth
  rescue method to restore breathing. Only trained
  persons should render this aid.

• Listen to the radio for news and instructions,
  including locations of emergency medical aid and
  holding areas for lost pets and livestock.

• Avoid storm-damaged areas.

• Be cautious of pets and other animals, contain your
  own pets and comfort them.

• Keep animals contained for a while.

• Repair broken windows, downed fences, fallen
  chimneys.

• Report downed power lines, sewer damage.

• If you are not at home , wait for confirmed reports
   on road damage and emergency routes before
   driving or returning home.

• Drive with caution, wait until the storm has passed.

BLIZZARDS

Winter is the time of year when most blizzards occur. Blizzards are common in the northern United States East of the Rocky Mountains, especially around the Great Lakes region, and in Canada. A blizzard is a tempestuous, frigid snow storm with blustery, piercing winds of 35 miles per hour or more and a windchill factor as low as below -20° Fahrenheit. Whiteouts are known to blind animals and people when the air is filled with so much snow that the earth and sky cannot be distinguished. Disorientation can drive livestock away from their quarters for long enough to freeze to death and human lives can be threatened by this phenomena as well. A blizzard can be a life-threatening event with the risk of hypothermia, frost bite, suffocation, and getting stranded. Potential dangers may be escalated by arctic conditions of temperatures as low as below zero degrees and winds of up to 100 miles an hour in mountainous regions.

Preparation for a blizzard includes winterizing and filling your car with gas, storing supplies and warm clothing in the home and car trunk, staying alert to storm warnings, and wearing layered clothing.

BEFORE THE BLIZZARD

OUTSIDE

It is best to stay inside, but if you must go out, take these precautions against the elements, frostbite, and hypothermia.

• Check insulation around exterior pipes.

• Layer up. Several lightweight layers of clothing provide more warmth than one heavy coat. Start with thermal underwear, add a turtleneck, a medium sweater, then a jacket.

• Wear a hat to prevent major heat loss. Cover your mouth so that your lungs are protected and wear gloves.

• Know the wind chill factor. Wind and very cold temperatures on skin can drive down your body temperature rapidly under these hazardous conditions.

• Be careful walking on snow and icy sidewalks. Wear heavy snow or hiking boots, golf shoes, or duct tape on the bottom of shoes. Sprinkle rock salt, sand, or kitty litter on slippery paths.

• Be sure to tell someone where you are going, your route, and your expected arrival time. In addition

to hypothermia and frostbite, getting stranded is
a real danger.

• Avoid driving the car if possible. Keep gas tank
  filled and keep fuel line from freezing.

• Keep supplies in the trunk of your car, including
  warm blankets, coats, gloves, hats and galoshes,
  shovel, sand, rope, tire chains, jumper cables, and
  bright signal cloth for the car's antenna.

• Have car winterized: flush radiator, add antifreeze.
  Other procedures may be indicated in a
  particularly cold climate.

• Check the battery and electrical system.

• Check headlights.

• Clear walking areas and uncover obstacles and
  fire hydrants, road signs, address numbers, street
  signs.

• Store firewood and check heating fuel supply, fill as needed.

INSIDE

• Store supplies and water.

• Secure your home.

• Take a First Aid and CPR class.

• Check and apply insulation around interior pipes.

• Wrap hot water heater.

• Have chimney flue cleaned out annually to prevent fire.

• Plan to conserve heat by shutting some rooms off or just heating one room.

• Insulate attic.

• Insulate around doors, windows, and outlets.

• Roll blankets or towels up and stuff under doors
  to block cold.

• Cover windows with storms windows, plastic, or
  shutters, hang with blankets or drapes.

DURING THE BLIZZARD

OUTSIDE

• Listen to portable radio for storm warnings.

• In case of a storm watch, be aware that a storm is
  possible.

- In case of a storm warning, head back towards shelter as a storm is headed for your area.

- In case of a blizzard warning, take shelter immediately.

- If you get stuck in the car, stay with the car.

- Tie the bright cloth onto the car's antenna for rescuers.

- Keep a window cracked for air.

- Keep your blood circulating and stay warm by moving your arms and legs while sitting.

- Start car once per hour, use heater for 10 minutes. Leave dome light on while engine runs.

• Check exhaust pipe, keep clear so exhaust fumes will not back up into car.

• Contain pets by leash or carrier.

INSIDE

• Keep a warm water faucet dripping to prevent frozen pipes.

• Monitor the storm on radio or TV.

• Gather stored supplies for use.

• Secure doors and windows.

• Ready blankets, dry warm clothing and hot water for those out in the storm.

- Prepare to give first aid for frostbite and hypothermia.

- Stay inside.

AFTER THE BLIZZARD

- Check for injuries and apply first aid.

- Approach pets with caution, comfort and aid them.

- Repair any broken waterpipes.

- Check chimney for structural damage and make repairs.

- Repair any broken windows.

- Call utility company to report downed power lines.

- Call 911 with any emergency requests or to get medical aid.

- Avoid storm-damaged areas.

- Check yard for damaged fencing or downed power lines before returning pets to the yard.

- Listen to radio for emergency information, including locations of holding areas for lost pets or livestock.

- Contain pets and livestock for a while.

TSUNAMIS

Japan has suffered the most tsunamis in the world. Tsunamis occur in the "Ring of Fire" in the Pacific Ocean.

A tsunami is literally a "harbor wave" and is known as a seismic sea wave because it can be caused by the shifting in the plates under the ocean, or by underwater volcanos and landslides. Tsunamis can erupt simultaneously with earthquakes, rocketing through water at breakneck speeds of up to 600 miles per hour. On top of the water the span between wave crests may measure up to 100 miles. In the open ocean, the wave is barely noticeable, but as the water becomes shallower near shore the wave rises and slows, growing to heights of as much as 200 feet. Tsunamis power into bays and river inlets, where they crash back and forth then tumble onto shore with explosive force.

Preparation for a tsunami will include Red Cross first aid classes, CPR training, evacuation and emergency training at the community level, storage of supplies, and awareness of changing tidal conditions and earthquakes that can signal a tsunami.

BEFORE THE TSUNAMI

OUTSIDE

• Drive or walk prearranged evacuation routes.

• Watch the ocean for sudden low tide and exposure of the ocean floor.

• Be aware of trembling ground and ground rolling up and down in waves.

- If you are in a boat at sea, stay at sea. Far from shore, you may only notice a slight rise in the water.

- If you are in a boat or ship near shore, put out to sea if a warning comes.

- Listen to the radio for tsunami warnings and evacuation instruction.

- If a tsunami watch is issued, an earthquake has been detected under the sea and a tsunami might occur.

- Go to high ground, even a cliff overlooking the ocean, and wait for further bulletins.

- If you hear civil defense sirens or your community signal, evacuate as trained.

- Do not approach the ocean. Always seek the highest ground you can.

- If you are in a bay or river inlet, be aware that tsunamis can grow very tall and dangerous in shallow water.

- Stay away from buildings that could topple.

- Stay away from bridges and other structures that could be washed away.

INSIDE

- Get insurance and document possession.

- Attend first aid and CPR classes.

- Attend Civil Defense and community meetings.

- Store supplies.

- Secure your home.

• Call family and neighborhood meetings.

• Listen to the radio for tsunami warnings and evacuation instructions.

• If a tsunami watch is issued, be aware that an earthquake has been detected under the sea and a tsunami might occur.

• Prepare to go to high ground and wait for further bulletins.

DURING THE TSUNAMI

• Stay away from buildings that could topple.

• Avoid bridges that could wash away.

• Complete evacuation procedures.

- Remain calm and wait for news and instruction.

- Contain dogs on leashes, cats in carriers.

- Stay at sea if you are at sea.

- Wait for the all-clear sirens or signal to return home.

AFTER THE TSUNAMI

- Check for injuries and render first aid.

- Do not return home until advised by authorities that conditions are safe.

- Check your home's exterior for chimney damage, separation of exterior walls, attachments, porches, and decks.

- Do not go inside the house if it looks unstable.

- If other family members are not there, follow your plan for locating one-another.

- Use your out-of-the-area contact person to relay messages. (It may take up to 3 days for the Red Cross to set up and convey information on specific persons.)

- Have a licensed inspector give an evaluation of the site for safety and insurance purposes.

- Approach animals with caution, contain your pets.

VOLCANOS

Volcanic eruptions are launched in "The Ring of Fire" in the Pacific Ocean where earthquakes and tsunamis are prevalent. Volcanos have erupted in Japan, the West Indies, Italy, and the United States. Kilauea, on the big island of Hawaii is one of the most active volcanos on earth. Elsewhere in the galaxy Mars, Neptune, and Jupiter all host volcanos.

Fifteen major pieces of the earth's crust called plates float on the hot molten layer below called the magma, much like pieces of crackers on a bowl of soup. One way a volcano is born is when two plates rub up against each other and piggyback so that one plate is plunged down into the molten inferno in the belly of the planet.

Fifty to sixty miles below the earth's crust, in the center of the earth, it is like a giant nuclear power plant, fueled by the breakdown of radioactive elements. The plummeting plate melts and shatters with such great velocity that pieces of rock are propelled up through the cracks in the earth's surface to burst forth in a fireworks of lava. When the lava rock hardens, it forms a mountain. Volcanic eruptions can also be touched off by earthquakes which occur in the middle of a plate

Preparation for a volcanic eruption will include documenting possessions, receiving first aid training, participating in community fire and evacuation drills, securing your home, preparing for earthquakes and wildfire, storing supplies and water, and being aware of earthquake predictions and procedures.

BEFORE THE ERUPTION

OUTSIDE

- If building a house in a forested area, contact the forestry department for recommendations on materials to use.

- Do not build near an active or dormant volcano.

- Use fire resistant materials when constructing a home, including treated wood products and aluminum.

- Plant trees and bushes sparsely to avoid a path of fuel for a fire due to lava flow.

- Tear off wood shake roof and replace with noncombustible roof.

• Landscape with low-growing plants.

• Use asphalt rag-roll roofing, tile, slate, cement
  shingle, sheet metal, or aluminum roofing
  materials.

• Trim trees away from roofs of home and garage
  or shop.

• Plant large trees a minimum of 10 feet from your
  home's exterior.

• Always water and prune the landscaping well so
  that it can serve as a protective fireline.

• Check the power lines to keep tree branches clear
  and call the utility company if trees are touching
  the wires.

• Generally maintain tree and shrub pruning and
  trimming.

- Haul away yard debris before it starts to pile up.

- Check to see that you are maintaining a 30 foot noncombustible, defensible space with no flammable vegetation in it all the way around your home as a fire break.

- If you live on a hillside or by a forest, you will need an additional clearing of up to 100 feet or more.

- Clean gutters and roof regularly to remove combustible leaves and needles.

- Follow local burning restrictions and safety requirements when disposing of debris.

- Store flammables away from the house.

- Stack firewood away from the house, not going down hill—fires often travel uphill.

• Have an adequate water supply to fight a fire.

• Fill and test large water tanks or cisterns, stand pipes, fire hydrants, or wells with high volume pumps.

• Prepare to access swimming pools, ponds, or storage tanks with portable pumps. Check working condition of equipment.

• In case of electrical failure, have an alternate power backup system for well pumps.

• Check water hoses to make sure they are long enough to reach all around the exterior of your home and test for leaks.

• Always keep a hose with a nozzle attachment connected to an outside outlet.

• Have a ladder tall enough to reach your roof.

• Stock standard fire fighting tools such as an axe, a rake, a chainsaw, a long-handled, round-point shovel and a 2 1/2 gallon water bucket.

• Guarantee emergency and firetruck access by maintaining two way roads with parking lanes.

• Build roads that slope less than ten feet per 100 feet to make the going easier for cumbersome firetrucks that have trouble with steep roads.

• Clear the roadway of flammable brush and materials 60 feet wide along the right of way to prevent wildfire hazard.

• In the event of imminent lava flow—leave the area. No man-made effort will stop molten rock.

INSIDE

- Get insurance and document your possessions.

- Attend community meetings on volcanos, earthquakes, and emergency evacuation procedures.

- Take Red Cross first aid, CPR, and fire safety classes.

- Call a family meeting and discuss where to go, what to take, where to meet if separated, what to do about pets.

- Plan escape routes—one by foot and two by car.

- Know where you will go and what you will take in case of evacuation.

- Store emergency supplies, food, and water.

- Post by every phone the number to call in case of fire.

- Install portable smoke detectors outside every sleeping area and on every level of your home and in garage and workshop.

- Use button to test smoke alarms twice a year.

- Store extra smoke alarm batteries.

- Keep fire extinguishers in the kitchen and hallways, test and replace immediately if faulty.

- Conduct fire drills, including walking or driving evacuation routes.

- Draw a floor plan and find two ways to escape from every room and conduct drills.

- Get rope or chain ladders for upper stories and practice using.

DURING THE ERUPTION

- Turn off gas at the meter to avoid danger of explosion.

- Put on heavy shoes and protective clothing.

- Take your stored supplies and complete evacuation procedures.

- Listen to the radio for updates on the volcano.

- Do not return home until the eruption is declared over and the lava flow and fires have stopped.

- Prepare to travel on a confirmed route.

- If driving, use extreme caution and take only confirmed routes. Abandon your car if lava and fire encroaches and take a route away from the fire.

AFTER THE ERUPTION

- Assist others and render first aid as safety permits.

- Listen to the radio reports for confirmed information and instructions, including location of Red Cross Disaster Stations, shelters and animal holding areas.

- Use caution going home. Do not return unless advised by authorities that conditions are safe and roads are clear.

- If driving is necessary, drive with caution. Visibility may be very poor if it is raining volcanic ash, and mud slides and landslides can occur.

- Avoid volcano damaged areas and lava flow areas.

- Go to the Red Cross Disaster Station for emergency treatment.

- Check your home's exterior for damage and stability. If an earthquake has occurred, use due caution and follow procedures.

- Do not go inside if it appears unsafe.

- If other family members are not there, follow your plan for locating one another, including calling your out-of-the-area contact person.

- Approach animals with caution and comfort and contain them as much as possible.

- Check and repair fenced areas for animals.

- Temporarily contain pets and livestock.

- Beware of loose or dangling electrical wires. Do not touch.

- Check gas appliance connections for signs of gas leaks. Do not light a match.

CYCLONES

A cyclone is wind blowing from 20 to 50 miles per hour with a low pressure area revolving around it. When the low pressure area intensifies, it can extend to levels of the atmosphere as high as 30,000 feet. Like hurricanes, these storms are members of the tropical cyclone family. Big, lumbering, and tame with a breadth of 1,000 miles in diameter and a lifespan of one week, cyclones are born to proclaim cold and stormy weather. They deliver blizzards and prolonged, bitter periods of snow and rain to numerous favorite breeding grounds. In North America, this includes just east of the Rockies and in the central and northeast United States. In the southern hemisphere, they spawn vortexes over the Pacific Ocean to the east and south of Japan. Cyclones travel to the northeast, starting above frozen Siberia, then dumping frigid deposits of punishing winter weather on Japan and following their northeast track from there. Although cyclones do not always carry precipitation, they bring thunderstorms and showers in warm sectors and climates. Cyclones that begin in the Gulf of Mexico mobilize along the eastern coast and on to the North Atlantic Ocean and those that begin in Spain strike the Mediterranean and Europe. They form in the Indian Ocean around Australia as well. Here, the direction of the winds' rotation changes and they blow in a counterclockwise direction, circulating around the placid center called the eye of the storm.

Preparation for a cyclone will include getting insurance, documenting possessions and property, checking and restocking stored supplies periodically. Taking a first aid class, attending community meetings, securing the house, building a shelter or designating a safe place to ride out the storm, and listening to the radio for storm advisories and evacuation instructions will also be useful.

BEFORE THE CYCLONE

OUTSIDE

- Watch the weather, look for darkening skies, rising wind, rain torrents. Stay alert.

- If at the beach, watch for waves coming inland.

- Leave low-lying areas due to the danger of floods and high tides.

- If swimming or in a boat, get to shore and seek shelter. Secure the boat or evacuate it to a pre-designated safe area.

- Secure or take inside garbage cans, children's toys, lawn furniture, gardening tools, barbecues, or any object that could be hurled by the wind.

• Fill your car's gas tank with gas as service stations may be shut down by the storm due to damage or power failure.

• Check your portable radio for news and instructions.

• Board up windows, close shutters, or tape glass. Wind pressure can shatter large windows and flying debris can break smaller panes of glass.

• Contain livestock.

INSIDE

• Get insurance and document your possessions.

• Take First Aid and CPR classes, attend community meetings.

• Listen for storm advisories and warnings on TV and radio.

• Check your supplies, camping equipment, and emergency cooking equipment.

• Secure your home. Move valuables and your family to the side of the house away from the wind.

• Check flashlights, portable radios for fresh batteries.

• Store water before the supply can be contaminated. Plastic bottles, clean jugs, pots and pans, and even the bathtub can serve as receptacles.

• If you are in a mobile home, or in an R.V. park leave the premises when you hear the storm warning and go to a designated shelter.

• Evacuate according to instructions.

DURING THE CYCLONE

- If your home is on high ground and sturdy, stay in and wait out the storm.

- Beware of the eye, the calm center of the storm, as it passes overhead. The calm can last from two minutes to half an hour.

- If you have a basement or storm cellar, that is the place to wait out the storm.

- If you do not have a basement, go to the lowest floor of your home, away from windows or glass doors.

- Contain pets by leash or carrier.

AFTER THE CYCLONE

- Check for injuries and render first aid.

- Avoid driving if possible. If driving is necessary, drive with caution. Debris may be hazardous and roads can collapse if undermined. Landslides are also possible.

- Listen to your radio for information such as flood warnings, location of shelters and red cross stations.

- Go to Red Cross disaster stations for emergency medical attention.

- Stay away from disaster areas unless qualified to help. First aid and rescue workers will function best unhampered.

- Use caution when returning home.

• Beware of loose or dangling electrical wires. Report to police or power company.

• Report broken sewers and water mains to your utility company.

• Stay away from river banks and streams where flooding can occur. Cyclones moving inland may bring severe flooding.

• Keep animals contained for a while.

TYPHOONS

Typhoons are created close to the Equator. These hurricane-like storms in the western Pacific Ocean are spawned as tropical depressions, developing in the oceans between the latitudes of 5 and 20 degrees North and South, where the temperature of the sea is 80 degrees Fahrenheit or more. 'Typhoon' is a specific name for a general product called a tropical cyclone. Typhoons and all tropical cyclones are most common in warmer weather in summer and fall and have an average lifespan of around ten days. Typhoons' paths are guided by trade winds.

Preparation for a typhoon will include documenting possessions, getting insurance, storing supplies prior to typhoon season, taking a first aid class, attending community meetings, securing the house, building a shelter or delegating a safe space, and listening for storm advisories.

BEFORE THE TYPHOON

OUTSIDE

• Watch the weather, look for darkening skies, rising wind, rain torrents. Stay alert.

• If at the beach, watch for waves coming inland.

• Leave low-lying areas due to danger from high tides and flooding.

• If swimming or in a boat, get to shore and seek shelter. Secure the boat or evacuate it to a pre-designated safe area.

• Secure or take inside garbage cans, children's toys, lawn furniture, gardening tools, barbecues, or any object that could be hurled by the wind.

- Fill your car's gas tank with gas as service stations may be shut down by the storm due to damage or power failure.

- Check your portable radio for news and instructions.

- Board up windows, close shutters, or tape glass. Wind pressure can shatter large windows and flying debris can break smaller panes of glass.

- Contain livestock.

INSIDE

- Get insurance and document your possessions.

- Attend community meetings, take First Aid and CPR classes.

- Listen for storm advisories and warnings on TV and radio.

- Check your supplies, camping equipment, and emergency cooking equipment.

- Secure your home. Move valuables and your family to the side of the house away from the wind.

- Check flashlights, portable radios for fresh batteries.

- Store water before the supply can be contaminated. Plastic bottles, clean jugs, pots and pans and even the bathtub can serve as receptacles.

- If you are in a mobile home, leave the premises when you hear the storm warning and go to a designated shelter.

- Evacuate according to instructions.

DURING THE TYPHOON

- If your home is on high ground and your home is of solid construction or reinforced, stay in and wait out the storm.

- Beware of the eye, the calm center of the storm, as it passes overhead. The calm can last from two minutes to half an hour. The storm is not over yet.

- If you have a basement or storm cellar, that is the place to wait out the storm.

- If you do not have a basement, go to the lowest floor of your home, away from windows or glass doors.

- Contain pets by leash or carrier.

AFTER THE TYPHOON

- Check for injuries and render first aid.

- Avoid driving if possible. If driving is necessary, drive with caution. Debris may be hazardous and roads can collapse if undermined. Landslides are also possible.

- Listen to your radio for information such as flood warnings, location of shelters, and location of Red Cross Disaster Stations.

- Go to Red Cross disaster stations for emergency medical attention.

- Stay away from disaster areas unless qualified to help. First aid and rescue workers will function best unhampered.

- Use caution when returning home.

- Beware of loose or dangling electrical wires. Report to police or power company.

- Report broken sewers and water mains to your utility company.

- Stay away from river banks and streams where flooding can occur. Typhoons moving inland can bring severe flooding.

- Keep animals contained for awhile.

BIBLIOGRAPHY and RESOURCES

American Red Cross— contact your local chapter. Provides pamphlets, videotapes, First Aid Manuals, and pocket masks for CPR.

Battan, Louis J. *The Nature of Violent Storms.* Garden City, NY: Doubleday, 1961.

Cope, Vern. *The Oregon Earthquake Handbook.* Portland, OR: V. Cope, 1993.

Davies, Patti. *Disaster Planning For Your Pets.* Animal Rescue and Care Fund.

Erickson, Jon. *Violent Storms.* Blue Ridge Summit, PA: TAB Books, 1988.

Federal Emergency Management Agency, *Helping Children Cope With Disaster.*

Federal Emergency Management Agency
Federal Center Plaza, 500 C Street, SW
Washington, DC 20472

Felknor, Peter S. *The Tri-State Tornado.*

Guide to Help You Prepare for the Next Quake, Part 1. *Sunset,* October 1990: 163–177.

Guide to Help You Prepare for the Next Quake, Part 2. *Sunset,* November 1990: 132–139.

Lampton, Christopher. *Forest Fire, a Disaster Book.* Brookfield, CT: Millbrook, 1991.

——. *Hurricane, A Disaster Book.* Brookfield, CT: Millbrook, 1991.

——. *Volcano, A Disaster Book.* Brookfield, CT: Millbrook, 1991.

Sloane, Eric. *The Book of Storms.*

Index

ORDER FORM

Name _____

Address _____

City/State/Zip _____

Phone _____

Enclosed is my check for $17.95 ($14.95 +$3 shipping & handling) for *SURVIVING NATURAL DISASTERS.*

DIMI PRESS
3820 Oak Hollow Lane, SE
Salem, OR 97302-4774

Phone **1-800-644-DIMI(3464)** for orders
or 1-503-364-7698 for further information
or FAX to 1-503-364-9727
or by INTERNET to dickbook@aol.com

Call toll-free and order now!

OTHER DIMI PRESS PRODUCTS FOR YOU

TAPES are available for... **$7.95** each

> **#1-LIVE LONGER, RELAX**
> **#2-ACTIVE RELAXATION**
> **#3-CONQUER YOUR SHYNESS**
> **#4-CONQUER YOUR DEPRESSION**
> **#5-CONQUER YOUR FEARS**
> **#6-CONQUER YOUR INSOMNIA**
> **#7-CONQUER YOUR CANCER**
> **#8-LAST LONGER, ENJOY SEX MORE**
> **#9-WEIGHT CONTROL**
> **#10-STOP SMOKING**
> **#11-LIVE LONGER, RELAX (female voice)**
> **#12-ACTIVE RELAXATION (female voice)**
> **#13-UNWIND WHILE DRIVING**
> **#14-RELAX AWHILE**
> **#15-RELAX ON THE BEACH/MEADOW**
> **#16-HOW TO MEDITATE**

TAPE ALBUM has six cassettes and is titled:

> **GUIDE TO RELAXATION** **$29.95**

BOOKS:

> **HOW TO FIND THOSE HIDDEN JOBS** gives tips
> on searching for a job...**$13.95**
>
> **SABOTAGE FLIGHT** is a Young Adult adventure story
> that takes place in the air over Alaska.......................**$9.95**
>
> **BUILD IT RIGHT!** is a book of advice on what to
> watch out for as you build your own home...........**$16.95**
>
> **FEEL BETTER! LIVE LONGER! RELAX** is a manual
> of relaxation techniques & a history of relaxation.**$9.95**
>
> **KOMODO, THE LIVING DRAGON (Rev. Ed.)**is the
> only account of the world's largest lizard **$14.95**
>
> **BLACK GLASS,** a hardcover novel about a gay man in
> the Merchant Marine at the time of Vietnam **$19.95**